ENTREPRENEURIAL FINANCE
A BEGINNERS GUIDE

Copyright © Startup Finance Limited.

ALL RIGHTS RESERVED

NO PART OF THIS BOOK MAY BE REPRODUCED IN ANY FORM, BY PHOTOCOPYING OR BY ANY ELECTRONIC OR MECHANICAL MEANS, INCLUDING INFORMATION STORAGE OR RETRIEVAL SYSTEMS, WITHOUT PERMISSION IN WRITING FROM THE PUBLISHER OF THIS BOOK.

ISBN 9798361797523

Authors: Nuno Arroteia and Bibek Bhatta

Second Edition.

Published Date 25/11/2021

Published by Startup Finance Limited

29 Commercial St, Dundee DD1 3DG, Scotland.

Email: esales@startup-finance.co.uk

Cover by Gangas Digital, Lda. using envato.elements

Printed in the United Kingdom

Preface

This book is intended to be a quick and useful guide to understanding and analysing the financial aspects of any business venture, particularly looking into its financial feasibility and profitability.

The feasibility and profitability of a business is not only a result of revenues. It is of course significant to generate sales, but businesses should also be analysed on how the balance between revenues and costs impacts the profits.

The examples provided in this book are designed to quickly and effectively introduce these key concepts so that the readers can immediately apply them to any project related to starting or expanding a business.

As the book is written in a way that discusses the fundamentals straightaway, it may not be suitable for someone expecting to gain an in-depth knowledge of aspects related to business finance and accounting.

This is also not an academic book. Despite using insights both from the authors' business experience and proven academic research, it is written without adopting the formality and rigidity of academic writing.

Therefore, its reduced size should fit the needs of speed and effectiveness that most entrepreneurs nowadays require.

In short, this book helps the readers to get a clear and straightforward understanding about:

- Evaluate the dynamics of start-up and growth stages of an entrepreneurial business venture and its relation to financial feasibility.
- Analyse and discuss critically the need, sourcing, and adequacy of different resources to support the financial feasibility across different stages of organisational growth.

- Critically assess and discuss the feasibility and scalability of a new venture integrating strategic management, operational management, and financial management.

The book starts with an explanation of key concepts related to designing a business model, looking at your business from a customer's perspective, and planning the essential resources you need to have in place to start the business. Subsequently, it introduces you to key information about costs and revenues, how they influence the margins of a business and, ultimately, its profitability. It also provides some insights on how to establish pricing strategies which, in turn, determine the revenues generated by the firm.

The break-even analysis is adopted to test a business's economic and financial feasibility, and extensive examples of how this method can be applied to testing a business model are presented. Towards the end, the book introduces techniques that are useful to define a cash-based budget which then can be used to anticipate cash flows of the business as well as to determine funding gaps and needs, and also introductory aspects about the legal framework to set up a business in the UK.

We are hopeful that the readers will find the time spent reading and thinking about the concepts explored in this book to be worthwhile. We wish you the best of reading and the best of luck in your venture!

If you want to keep updated with other publications in this collection, please visit our website (www.startup-finance.co.uk) and drop us an e-mail to receive updates.

Wish you all the best,

Nuno and Bibek

Contents

1. **Designing a business model** 7
   1.1. Identifying your customers 10
   1.2. Predicting revenues 13
   1.3. Estimating the resources 20
2. **Testing the business feasibility** 27
   2.1. Understanding business profitability 27
   2.2. What are costs 31
   2.2.1. Fixed costs 33
   2.2.2. Variable costs 34
   2.2.3. Cost structure 36
   2.2.4. Fixed and variable costs per unit 37
   2.3. What are revenues 39
   2.3.1. Cost-based or mark-up pricing 41
   2.3.2. Market-based pricing 42
   2.3.3. Competitor-based pricing 43
   2.3.4. Pricing strategies for the long term 44
   2.4. What are margins 48
3. **Calculating the Break-Even point** 51
   3.1. Simulating different scenarios 54
   3.2. Testing the operational capacity 57
   3.3. A temporal perspective for the BEP 59

3.4.	Defining profitability objectives	60
3.5.	Further examples	61
3.5.1.	Example 1 - Counselling practice	61
3.5.2.	Example 2 - Online retailer	64

4. Building a financial model (Budget, P&L, and Cash flow statements) 69

4.1.	Master budget	71
4.2.	Cash-based budgeting	77
4.2.1.	Capital and Operating expenditures	82
4.3.	Profit and Loss statement	84
4.4.	Determining the funding needs for the business	88

5. Financial KPIs: Payback, IRR, NPV 95

6. Simulating the financial impacts of decision-making 105

7. Legal Structure of a business 111

8. Bibliography 119

9. Remissive index 121

1. Designing a business model

A business model is a framework by which to operate your business, as centred on your value proposition and alignment with the market and supported by endogenous and exogenous resources in the firm. A successful business model in the long term means that you can generate profits that (partially or fully) can be reinvested in the firm, its resources and growth.

A business model starts with a value proposition and the identification of your desired customers with whom you wish to establish commercial relationships. However, how exactly will you reach out to your customers? What channels will you be using to communicate your offer to them? Will you be contacting customers regularly and, if so, will you be using primarily social media, cold calls, participation in industry or networking events, trade fairs and exhibitions, conferences, etc?

Therefore, an important aspect of the development of the business model is the representation of your customer's journey. The customer journey is the complete sum of experiences (and actions) that customers go through when interacting with your company.

Instead of looking at just a part of a transaction or experience, the customer journey documents the full experience of being a customer.

It is, therefore, important, that you reflect on how the customer experiences your product from when they first get to know it until they buy it, and what additional support you offer (after-sales). By no means is a customer experience just a transactional moment in time when you exchange goods for money, and nowadays it is vital to create a long-term relationship and understanding with your customer. But why should this be important?

The main reason is so-called customer retention. As you may now have noted, it takes a lot of time and effort to get one paying customer on board (some start-up businesses never actually manage to get to that stage), so why should you then necessarily let the customer go after one successful transaction? Indeed, your goal should be to have the customer repeat the purchase.

This implies that the cost of acquiring a customer is diluted if they buy from you more than once. It has also a positive impact in terms of potentially minimising the probability of the customer being diverted to your competitors. Moreover, a happy customer is more likely to endorse your products to others, therefore they will be effectively working for you at no cost and can lead to potential new opportunities.

Business models can change. This is a fact. You will see that you will make changes to your business model as you start your business and in its subsequent growth. However, fundamentally changing a business model is increasingly difficult, particularly as the firm gets bigger. In this sense, take your time to reflect on your business model, look at your competitors and learn from them before committing to decisions.

On the other hand, having a solid idea of your business model to start with will help you to better understand which aspects of the business you should focus on at specific times, and what aspects and functions you may need to change or adapt. Nonetheless, as it is dynamic, changing something related to one element will inevitably have an impact on the whole model, and is up to you and your team to find an adequate way to manage this balance.

To convey an initial draft of your business model, fill in your answers to the questions (next table). In doing so, you are already reflecting on and building an initial working version.

Business model

Value proposition and customer fit	Is the value proposition aligned with the customers' gains and pains? Do you know how you will convey your offer to the customer and maximise the prospects of customer retention?
Who your customers are	Do you know who your customers are and why they will be willing to buy from you?
Internal resources and value proposition fit	Do you have the internal resources required to ensure that you deliver the value proposition? What internal activities and processes do you have in place and how critical are they to fulfilling the value proposition?
External resources (and partners) and value proposition fit	Do you have/need to have other resources external to the business such as suppliers and/or business partners to help you to deliver the value proposition to the customers? Are your external partners aligned with your expectations, concerns and beliefs to avoid failure in meeting customers' expectations?

1.1. Identifying your customers

As noted, it is vital to start with a clear identification of who your customers are. The profile of your customer is sometimes referred to in the literature as the customer persona; a fictional character who embodies the typical profile of a customer (or more than one customer in case you need to create a different persona for each). It is a generalised representation of your ideal customer.

A customer persona is a more human view (albeit fictional) of your market segment as it embodies aspects related to human behaviours, motivations, and needs, beyond just demographic, social and/or economic characteristics. which is a vital step in preparing your further actions to approach potential customers.

Customer personas help you to understand your customers better and make it easier for you to tailor content to their specific needs, behaviours, and concerns. Personas are based on market research as well as on insights you gather from an actual or prospective customer base (through surveys, interviews, etc.). Depending on your business, you could have as few as one or two personas, or as many as 10 or 20.

At the most basic level (and this is your starting point), personas allow you to personalise or target your marketing for different segments of your audience. For example, instead of sending the same lead nurturing emails to everyone in your database, you can segment by buyer persona and tailor your messaging according to what you know about those different personas.

It could be that your customers are not the end consumers, in which case you must also figure out how to reach out to the end consumers if they are vital to generating demand. As you might have guessed, it is also very different to establish communication channels with B2B customers compared to B2C, and this must be accounted for.

The next table presents the structure of the elements you should now focus on to build the persona of your main customer (use one table for each persona). Each persona represents a customer group or segment that can be targeted with different strategies and actions.

Create a customer persona

Persona name	
Who is your persona?	
Background (about them)	
Demographics (and other relevant segmentation attributes)	
Identifiers (communication preferences, demeanour, how they engage with businesses)	
What is the use case?	
Goals	
Challenges (pain points)	
What can you do to help (benefits)	
Why should they buy from you?	
Choice factors	
Buying trigger	
Buying process	
Common objections	

How will you get their attention?	
What do they look for in a business presentation?	
How are they contacted by sellers?	

Now it is time to start looking at the business from the perspective of your customer's journey. A way of starting is by identifying how your customers will look at your business from the moment they first get the information about your products, to the point where a decision was made concerning the product and eventually, its purchase, what support mechanisms you have to help the customer after-sales, and what can trigger the customer to decide to buy from you again.

The importance of mapping the customer journey is that it will help you to figure out the key resources that you need to have in place to deliver what you promise in your value proposition to your customer – this will be covered shortly ahead. See the example below to start mapping out the journey of your customer.

Map your customers' journey

Moments in time – the step-by-step experience of the customer concerning you/your business.	Touchpoint – map all the moments of interaction with the customer, how you contact the customer, the frequency, etc., and define actions to deal with all of them.	Blind moments – circumstances when your customer is not in touch but could think of contacting you (to ask for advice, information, repeat an order)
1		
2 ...		

1.2. Predicting revenues

Once you grasp a better understanding of who your customer or customers are and their journey, you can start working on planning the revenues (or sales) for your business, based on the quantification of the market size. One of the most critical and difficult aspects of starting a business is to forecast revenues. Revenues are of the utmost importance as they generate cash and profits without which the business cannot be sustained.

You should also be prepared for the fact that no forecasting is accurate as it will change as you start trading. However, this does not mean that it is not important to establish some assumptions and principles, subject to subsequent revisions and adjustments based on your learning and practice. And that is key to preparing you better for your business journey.

Forecasting is related to anticipating the revenues of the units of the output of the products or services which will be sold. This is highly complex, as few techniques will allow forecasting with accuracy, particularly when launching a new business in which there is no history or record of previous sales.

However, some guidelines can be used to establish a reasonable estimate of the number of units that can be potentially sold on the market. For that, you must start by quantifying the market in which you will be entering. Market quantification implies working out several customers, either individuals or businesses that could be potential buyers of the services or products sold by the firm.

This number represents the maximum number of customers, implying that all the competitors entering the same market will share them.

Unfortunately, a common mistake made by start-ups and growing businesses is aiming for an unrealistic number of target customers, and this can destroy any credibility of their business plans.

The advantage of quantifying the market size is that having done so makes it unlikely that the business will forecast revenue quantities that are much larger than the market it intends to serve in the first place. On the other hand, it avoids that you disregarding market potential and don't plan to scale up the business to maximize its growth potential.

The key to quantifying the market is access to quality and reliable information, and for that, you may want to start using secondary data sources such as newspaper articles, academic journals, public reports, statistics, and market research studies made by credible organisations. Therefore, quantifying the market will require searching online with keywords related to the characteristics of the target individual customers, such as their gender, social habits, geography, buying power, consuming habits, and trends.

As a rule of thumb, relying on only one source of information is not recommended. It would be more prudent to confront the data by comparing different sources; this is because there are likely to be differences among various sources. The objective of this approach is to get an estimate of the potential market size, and not an exact dimension as this will be almost impossible to accomplish.

As an example, let us assume that the GAME Company has identified that the total market size in the UK for board games is 500,000 potential buyers per year. Naturally, the firm will not attain a 100% market share at the start as there are other competitors already on the market; therefore, it is reasonable to estimate a much lower percentage at the entry stage.

The next table exemplifies how different market shares can be simulated for different scenarios depending on how optimistic or pessimistic the firm is.

Examples of market quantification

Market size estimate (UK)	Potential market share	Number of units sold
500,000 individual buyers	1%	5,000
	5%	25,000
	10%	50,000

A bigger market does not necessarily mean a better opportunity as you might not be able to mobilise enough resources to compete with others. Trust us, if the market is big enough there will be others stepping on your doorstep to get in as well, no matter how much you think you might be better prepared or protected from competitors. Big businesses always have the money and resources to allocate to new promising markets, whereas start-ups do not.

Now that you have started, let's calculate the Total Addressable Market (TAM) for your product. TAM is the overall revenue opportunity available or foreseen for a specific product or service, considering any future expansion scenarios. Assessing the TAM is crucial for start-ups as well as existing enterprises because this estimate allows them to prioritise the available markets, customer segments, products and business opportunities by comparing the potential for revenue generation and profits. Finally, it leads to a viable value proposition offering to potential business investors and buyers.

To know your TAM, you should start by estimating the number of customers in your market. For this, you will use a combination of top-down and bottom-up analysis. A top-down analysis starts by using secondary market research to determine how many end-users meet different characteristics.

An example of calculating a TAM with a top-down analysis might be as follows. If you have developed a technology that revolutionises the toothpaste industry by improving the efficacy of toothpaste to prevent cavities and other tooth-related diseases.

For example, if an average person brushes their teeth twice per day, and this is most frequent in developed and developing economies, there are 3 billion people in the world that fall into this category (the numbers are not accurate but just to convey the example). On average, a toothpaste tube is enough for 30 uses and costs $2 which means that each time someone brushes their teeth it costs 0.06(7) pence.

Therefore, the TAM would be calculated as follows:

> *TAM = 3 billion people x 2 (brush teeth twice a day) x 0.067 (cost per each brush) x 365 days in a year = $146,730,000,000.00*

A quite large market isn't it? Now imagine that you could potentially get a share of just about 1% of that!

Use the process map below to estimate the number of customers and their buying patterns and frequency.

Top-down estimate of the number of customers

Segment	Sources	Data/Information
Start with a broader segment, for example, how many customers you estimate belong to the market segment that you identified as being the most relevant. Customers can be individuals or organisations alike.	What sources of information have you used to identify the number of customers?	What is the data that you came up with? What are the assumptions for your calculations (if applicable)?
Refine your segmentation. What assumptions do you have to make to narrow down the list of customers by looking at more specific criteria or characteristics they may have?	What sources of information have you used to identify the number of customers?	What is the data that you came up with? What are the assumptions for your calculations (if applicable)?
Repeat the procedure until you get to a segment size which you think is more tangible, objective, and reachable compared to where you started.	What sources of information have you used to identify the number of customers?	What is the data that you came up with? What are the assumptions for your calculations (if applicable)?

A top-down analysis should be complementary to a bottom-up one. This approach is different from the previous one as it departs from a granular level of analysis to find waypoints that are extrapolated up to the wider population. It is more practical to conduct a bottom-up analysis if you have already a business up and running, which is not currently the case for you.

However, a good way to approach this is as follows. Using the case of one potential customer (or ideally) more than you have contacted, identify – specifically – what the number of sales that this customer could potentially generate is, and why. From there, you can extrapolate that to other similar customers who, if buying from you, could generate a similar multiple in your sales. You would therefore have to extrapolate to an entire market, departing from the regional to the country level and international.

A bottom-up analysis is by no means an easy task. The goal is that you can identify the TAM using the two distinct analyses and compare them to see which one is more credible. You should not blend them but look at what aspects make sense (or not), and ideally, come up with a TAM estimate that is consistent with both approaches. But avoid "meeting in the middle", as this is generally not a good solution.

Please be aware that the TAM is an estimation and is very difficult to guess with precision. The more credible your data sources are and the more your assumptions make sense, the better the estimate might be. Also, try to get some data from your competitors to see if your findings make sense.

Now, how can you estimate your potential market share from the overall TAM cake? Your market share or percentage of the overall market is called the SAM or Serviceable Available Market. The SAM is the portion of the TAM that a given business is servicing. Using the previous example, let's assume that you would start selling your toothpaste technology in the USA. The global market is the TAM, whereas the USA is the SAM.

The SAM gives you a much better sense of how many sales you can make with your product, but the TAM is useful in indicating how much room there is for potential growth.

> **SAM = % of TAM you can realistically obtain**

On the other hand, it is also unlikely that you will become the sole supplier in the USA (even if your technology is the best), as not all players will be willing to buy from you, thus limiting the scalability of the internal market.

Hence, the SOM, or Serviceable Obtainable Market, is the portion of the SAM you can realistically capture. And this is the market size that in the end, you should consider figuring out the sales volume that you can expect to achieve when starting a business.

> **SOM = % of SAM you can realistically obtain**

See the picture below for an example of the TAM, SAM, and SOM.

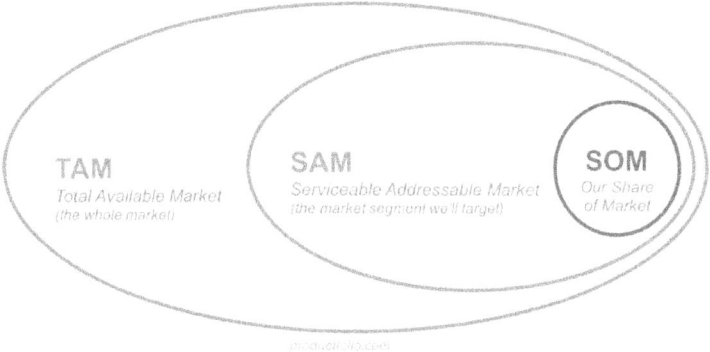

1.3. Estimating the resources

Now it is time to look at the resources that you must have to be able to deliver and sell your product to your market (SOM). By support structure, we mean the firm-level resources and capabilities which you probably don't yet have, but you will need to think ahead as you might end up needing them in the future.

Human resources – Critical to the success of any organisation are its human resources, beyond you, which you may have to get on board to help you with various business functions, such as marketing, sales, manufacturing, operations, etc. What profiles should they have, where you will recruit them, and how will you train them and ensure that they have the resources they need to do their best?

Recruitment and training choices allow you to manage your workers to get the most out of the hours that they work, whilst the provision of equipment supports each worker in carrying out their functions. There are 2 different types of a worker:

- Employees - People employed directly by the company, permanently assigned to a job function.
- Contract Workers - Temporary workers. They cost a lot more than permanent employees, but they can be brought in easily when needed, and out when not needed.

If a business doesn't have enough internal resources to carry out the specified work then it will try to recruit more workers as employees or contract workers. These are important decisions to make before you start or grow a business, to avoid not being able to deliver what you promise to your customers as you don't have enough resources to handle the different processes and activities.

Concerning human resources is also important to understand what motivates people to work for and with you and your business, which is far more than just the salary. Some aspects that you should consider besides the number of resources and what you will pay them are (but not are limited to): morale/satisfaction as a measure of happiness in the job; how much overtime is required and what rate of overtime is paid; the quality of your premises and workplace; the salary level of the workers; the level of training to be provided.

The negative effect of these factors will be immediately apparent in a reduction in motivation by the human resources, with a negative impact on their productivity and potentially leaving the company.

Premises, equipment, and IT – You should also consider selecting the premises within which your business functions are carried out. Particularly if your business is not an online business, you may need to have dedicated premises to run the business activity and to meet customers, or to deal with other processes (such as stocks and logistics for example). Most companies need to change premises as they grow but the preference is always to make planned rather than forced moves.

Even if your business is 100% online, you still require thinking through how your website must be built, the capacity to accommodate traffic without delays, broadband speed to access the Internet and other communications, and security aspects to prevent others from inappropriately accessing your data, just to name a few.

If your business involves manufacturing then you should look at other aspects such as the space available, the equipment to use, power supply, layout, lighting, and safety and security issues. Equipment is whatever is needed by the workers to carry out their tasks. Typical items of equipment would be furniture, communications, computers, copiers, etc. An adequate floor area is required to provide the space for all your business activities to be carried out efficiently and to store components and product stock.

Whilst you can make assumptions at any one time you should also consider any future changes in your requirements, for example considering whether your premises are enough to accommodate future growth or if you may need to relocate.

Key processes and activities – To provide a service and/or sell a product there are key processes that cannot be unaccounted for. Every business has different critical processes, and those you should be primarily focused on, whilst leaving those processes that are not essential (but important) to work as a second priority.

The following section summarizes some processes and activities that are typical in most commercial organizations to help you to identify the ones that are more critical in your case. It could be that all of them are critical, or that just a few are more important; however, you must differentiate those that cannot fail from those that are less vital and that may underperform without affecting the value and delivery of your value proposition to the market.

1) **Marketing and sales** – This includes all the processes and activities that raise the customer's awareness about your product,

drive them to engage with you and potentially buy from you, whilst also providing after-sale service and mechanisms to ensure customer satisfaction and retention. The marketing and sales function includes, but is not limited to:

a) Market Research - Gain the maximum amount of market intelligence whilst minimizing the time and cost involved in gathering research.

b) Branding - Create a brand that encompasses key selling points/value propositions that you want your company and its products to be synonymous with.

c) Pricing - Set a price that is attractive to customers, compares well to the competition and allows for a profit to be made.

d) Promotions - Find the most cost-effective way to create demand for your product and awareness of your brand.

e) Sales Channels - Gain maximum exposure for your product whilst minimizing the amount of time and size of the discount you need to encourage channels to take up your product(s). Examples of sales channels are online websites, wholesalers, retailers, or your shop and premises.

2) **Operations** – This includes all the processes and activities that deliver the service to your customer. In manufacturing environments, it covers not only the production but also the sourcing/purchasing of the materials and the logistics to transport the goods to the sales channels or deliver them to the customers. The operations function includes, but is not limited to:

a) Purchasing - Ensure that enough components are ordered to allow you to complete your production run.

- b) Production - Ensure that you have enough products to meet demand at any time and keep costs low enough to allow you to make enough profit to sustain your business.
- c) Quality Control - Monitor the quality of your products before they reach the customer.
- d) Logistics - Manage the process of getting your products to your customers.

3) **Research and development** – This includes all the processes and activities that allow you to maintain your competitive edge and leadership on the market, by investing in ongoing research and product development and/or design.

4) **Support services** – These are often considered less vital but still play an important role in running a business and include for example the accounting and legal services that you may need software and communications to work with the computers, cleaning, or security services. Of course, the support services vary for each business and depend on the nature of the business itself.

Partners – As in any business, you will not be entirely dependent on yourself and your internal resources, but also on external parties. In this sense, it is also important to reflect on your suppliers (existing or future), as the growth of your business might dictate that you must rely on others to support you instead of producing everything internally. For obvious reasons, you will most likely rely on external suppliers such as professional services firms to deliver you help with law, contracts, accounting and tax reporting, or even social media and marketing campaigns.

But when it comes to the main product, the core of what your company does, will you rely on third parties to supply all or parts of it, or will you decide to manufacture the different elements or activities related to your product internally in their entirety? This is a vital decision that you must also consider at this stage.

We would not advise you to outsource critical elements of your product or service at this stage, as you will lose control and potentially expose yourself too much to the market and potential competitors. But, on the other hand, you might not have all the resources that you may need to fulfil the production internally. There is a trade-off between outsourcing and insourcing. Outsourcing is the process of hiring an outside organisation that is not affiliated with the company to complete specific tasks. Insourcing, on the other hand, is a business practice performed within the operational infrastructure of an organisation.

However, partners are not just suppliers. You may have to have other partners that are neither suppliers nor customers, but that can mediate the way to access better suppliers or better customers. In this sense, partners can be any individual or organisation that performs a key role in assisting your organisation to reach its market and/or to optimise its internal processes and procedures. See some examples below:

1) **Business incubators and accelerators –** There is a wide range of offers everywhere in the world of business incubators (either privately owned or of a university or research setting), with acceleration programs sometimes offered by the business

incubators themselves, and a wide array of services that come with it, supposedly to help you to start your own business.

2) **Mentors** – identify a suitable mentor to help you move forward with your market research. This can be someone that you already know and have worked with, someone working for the same organisation as you or someone whom you came across in your life that you trust and feel has the expertise needed to support you going forward at this stage. This could be a co-worker, a former colleague, a former boss, or even a former teacher or supervisor.

3) **Business angels and private investors** – Business angels are private investors who don't just spend their time with you for the sake of your beautiful eyes, but because they might see some potential in your business idea and want (possibly) to invest in your business, whilst in return, they expect to exploit the financial benefits of being co-owners of a successful business.

4) **Getting on with a business partner** – An individual partner can be helpful, particularly if it is someone who already has had some business experience or is (ideally) launching a business (not necessarily a science-based business though).

2. Testing the business feasibility

This chapter focuses on important aspects of your business related to its feasibility in the medium- to long term. You have already developed an initial business model and identified the key resources that you need to have in place to run your business. Now is the time to move on towards a better understanding of the financial side of starting a business.

2.1. Understanding business profitability

Let us now discuss some aspects related to profitability and why it is so important at this stage. In this section, we will guide you through some of the principles related to testing the financial feasibility of your business. They are not meant to be a bulletproof financial plan at this stage, but we have decided to include them here so that you can start to gain a feel for how important it is to think right now about the financial side of your business.

We want you to take the next steps carefully, as you are probably not familiar with business finance and accounting and it could be that you feel you don't have all the information needed to move on with some of the necessary calculations. Which you don't!

However, please try your best, and use all the information that you can to see whether you might be on the right track to a profitable business. From my own experience, many entrepreneurs, and mostly those from STEM backgrounds, with no specific business knowledge fail to test their businesses in their early stages, only to find out that investors ask them questions about this, for which they are then entirely unprepared. This, for obvious reasons, puts off potential investors no matter how interesting your product might be.

On the other hand, it is important to prepare yourself and to understand in depth the profitability of a business from an early start, as its results may force you to make drastic changes to the business model from which you had planned to initiate the business, or even, in extreme circumstances, force you to discard a specific solution, market segment, or both which may become unattainable, in favour of other which can bring profit in the future.

Any organisation, regardless of its intent to generate profit or not, needs to be managed in such a way that at least it makes enough revenue to be able to pay for its costs. The sources of revenue can vary depending on the type of organisation, and whether it is profit-oriented or not. For a public-sector organisation, such as a public service, hospital, or university, most of the revenues are generated by public funding, and secondarily by user fees. For a charity or any other kind of non-governmental organisation, the income would come from a mix of public funding, private donations, and user fees. For a business, most of the revenue is generated by selling its products and services to the market/paying customers.

Profitability is the primary goal of a business due to the following principal reasons:

- A profitable business tends to be sustainable in the long term;

- A profitable business generates returns to pay for the initial investments made, hence allowing investors to recover the capital invested in the business;
- A profitable business generates profits that can be paid to the shareholders (owners), managers, and employees, thereby increasing their commitment towards working for and supporting the firm;
- A profitable business enables the firm to invest in its future growth and depend less on other sources of money such as lenders or external investors.

Profitability can be measured by subtracting the costs (of resources used and consumed) from the revenues generated by business activities. Hence, to be profitable, a business must create a surplus, or a positive difference, when costs are subtracted from revenues.

The profitability of a business can be checked from the income statement, which is a summary statement of revenues and costs during a defined accounting period (usually one year).

Our approach to helping you to understand profitability will be achieved via the analysis of operational profits, which in turn refers to the difference between operating revenues and costs (i.e., revenues and costs related to usual business activities).

It should be noted at the outset that profitability must not be mistaken for liquidity or the availability of cash; a business may be profitable according to its income statement but may not have enough money available to meet its immediate obligations. Hence, there is a big difference between profitability and cash flows, but we will come back to this later.

By definition, a firm is profitable if it can generate surpluses from its operational activities, therefore creating gains on top of the costs needed to support its operations.

In simple mathematical terms, profit can be represented as follows:

> **Profit = Total Revenue – Total Costs**

There are two key aspects to this equation, namely revenue and cost. To generate profit, a business must generate revenue; and to increase its profitability in absolute terms, it needs to maximise the positive difference between revenues and costs.

It is paramount to keep costs under control because costs tend to increase with increasing sales. Therefore, the costs must be managed so that they do not grow at a faster pace than sales; otherwise, the benefits of generating more revenue would not compensate for the costs of resources needed to attain them. The consequence would be an unsustainable revenue growth trajectory which could endanger the future of the business.

Understanding the concepts of costs, revenues, and margins is crucial to managing any business effectively.

2.2. What are the costs

Cost can have multiple meanings depending on the context. Hence, it is usual for the term cost to be preceded by another associated term; for example, direct costs, indirect costs, fixed costs, variable costs, etc.

Cost, in a narrow sense, can be defined as the money spent by a firm to generate operating revenue.

A firm may need to pay wages and utility bills which are easily recognisable as costs, whereas other costs like depreciation may not be so evident because firms would not usually 'pay' for depreciation.

First, it is essential to understand the difference between direct costs and indirect costs.

Direct costs are those costs that can be exclusively and accurately traced to a particular cost object.

Cost object in this sense refers to any activity of interest for which cost needs to be measured: it could be a product, a service, a mix of products, a business division, and so forth. For example, if business owners are interested in measuring the cost of a product that the business produces - such as a simple testing kit to verify the presence of a disease by analysing a sample of human blood (cost object) - the materials needed to make it can be considered a direct cost.

However, the rent paid for the premises where the factory is located would be difficult to assign to the production of testing kits accurately if the firm manufactures other products as well. Hence, the rent in such cases would be an indirect cost as far as the manufacturing cost of the testing kits is concerned. While calculating the manufacturing cost of the cost object, such indirect costs also have to be allocated to the cost object reasonably.

Based on the value proposition, functions, and features of your product, you should now briefly try to identify the direct costs associated with making and delivering one unit of your product. Start with the following:

Direct cost allocation

Name of the cost object	Measuring units	Cost rubrics
Complete one line for each product (if applicable)	Could be in time (in case of a service), weight, size, single individual unit, pack of more than one unit	Sales commissions paid to agents Direct materials and direct labour Production supplies for the manufacturing of goods Electricity, gas, and water consumed (beyond the minimum, recurring base charges) Extraordinary repair and maintenance costs

Regarding how the level of activity influences costs, they can also be divided into fixed or variable costs.

2.2.1. Fixed costs

Fixed costs (also known as overheads) tend to remain generally the same in the short term (for example one year) whereas variable costs tend to change with the level of output (such as sales). In the following section, we will discuss these differences further.

Fixed costs tend to remain the same regardless of the firm's output which can be measured regarding the number of units produced, as well as the number of units sold (which can be considered a proxy to a cost object).

That is precisely why fixed costs are so significant, because a firm cannot avoid them and, therefore, the business needs to generate sufficient sales volume to pay for them.

Fixed costs are also generally difficult to assign to products or services, especially if the firm produces more than one product or line of service. Hence, fixed costs are also referred to as indirect costs or overheads.

More importantly, fixed costs are recurrent: incurred every week, month, or year. Besides, fixed costs are not dependent on having a certain number of customers or the level of goods or services being produced or sold. This means that the firm still must pay the rent even if it does not manage to sell anything!

All businesses have fixed costs no matter how small or big they are.

Here are some examples of fixed costs:

- Accounting and Legal
- Utilities
- Insurances
- Office supplies
- Interests
- Rent of the premises
- Foreseeable repair and maintenance
- Salaries and wages
- Marketing

Fixed costs are usually dependent on the installed capacity of the business regarding its maximum output; therefore, it is contingent upon a given operational level.

Installed capacity refers to the maximum production capacity, such as the number of units that can be produced by the business during a specific period (usually one year), or the number of units sold. Hence, a decision to increase capacity in response to demand fluctuations, whether permanently or temporarily, could make the firm incur higher fixed costs.

2.2.2. Variable costs

As the term itself suggests, variable costs vary depending on the output of a business; this means that such costs tend to rise as production or sales (or both) increase and tend to decrease conversely.

In contrast to fixed costs, variable costs can usually be linked to the units of outputs/costs objects and, therefore, are considered direct costs.

Below are some examples of variable costs:

- Sales commissions paid to agents
- Direct materials and direct labour
- Production supplies for the manufacturing of goods
- Electricity, gas, and water consumed (beyond the minimum, recurring base charges)
- Extraordinary repair and maintenance costs

For example, in most businesses, making and selling more product units per day increases the variable costs (direct) due to higher consumption of utilities (such as electricity and gas), amenities, or breakfasts served.

Additionally, some costs can be described as semi-variable costs or semi-fixed costs, also known as semi-fixed costs. These are composed of a mixture of fixed and variable components; hence, they are fixed for a set level of output and become variable after the threshold is exceeded.

A typical example would be that of a mobile phone contract where a fixed amount of fee needs to be paid each month as long as the associated monthly allowance is not exceeded; however, the customer would have to pay extra if they exceed the monthly call time or data allowance, where this additional payment depends on the level of excess services used by the customer.

2.2.3. Cost structure

Classifying a cost as fixed or variable is determined based on whether it fluctuates with the volume of output (which can be measured by the number of units produced or sold).

If the cost increases when the output increases, then it is a variable cost, whereas if it remains constant regardless of the change in output, then it is a fixed cost. It is, therefore, critical to know how the costs change as sales increase or decrease.

The total costs of running a business for a given period are the sum of total fixed costs and total variable costs.

Hence, the total cost structure can be mathematically represented as follows:

> **Total Costs = Total Fixed Costs + Total Variable Costs**

Therefore, it is always imperative to reflect on the cost structure before starting up or expanding a business.

Different businesses have different cost structures, which makes it very difficult to identify the correct amount of costs that can be considered healthy. Therefore, the break-even analysis which will be developed below can be useful.

However, as a rule of thumb, it is essential to consider that the higher the fixed costs, the worse for the business: the consequence of high fixed costs is that the company will have to pay for them regardless of having any sales or otherwise.

On the other hand, higher variable costs will only be incurred by a business as and when sales are generated.

Notwithstanding the importance of managing the cost structure throughout all the stages of the business growth, it is particularly important to pay attention to this at the start of the business when the availability of initial funds may be limited as compared to an ongoing established business.

Therefore, it should be considered beforehand whether the firm has sufficient cash to cover the fixed costs for at least the first year of operations, otherwise, this could cause severe problems such as disruption of the business activities in the short term.

2.2.4. Fixed and variable costs per unit

Fixed costs are relatively easy to forecast as they are more likely to be known in advance, whereas variable costs can be more difficult to anticipate as they are generally less predictable and more challenging to measure.

After all, variable costs depend on the volume of the output which in turn depends upon many other factors. For example, changing the number of units produced by a business can influence the quantity and costs of materials consumed, as well as extra hours of labour needed. From a practical perspective, it can be difficult to estimate the variable costs per unit of output.

NANO Company produces functional inks for a varied range of B2B customers. It anticipates that its yearly fixed costs are $200,000 and that the firm plans to produce 100,000 litres at peak capacity. Even though total fixed costs do not change, the amount of fixed costs per unit tends to decrease with the increase in the number of units produced, i.e., the more board game units produced, the lower the fixed costs per unit.

For example:

Total fixed costs	Production (number of units)	Fixed costs per unit
$200,000	10	$20,000
$200,000	100	$2,000
$200,000	500	$400

However, the variable costs per unit produced remain the same. For example, let us consider that the company has a variable cost of $5 to produce one litre.

The variable cost per unit remains the same, but the total variable cost depends on the number of units produced, as illustrated below:

Variable costs per unit	Production (number of units)	Total variable costs
$5	10	$50
$5	100	$500
$5	500	$2,500

Therefore, the total fixed cost remains constant but the fixed cost per unit changes with the variation regarding the units of production, and the variable cost per unit remains constant but the total variable cost changes with the number of units produced.

The unit variable cost may also decrease with the increase in production as a buyer will be able to command a better price at more favourable terms from the supplier; however, we will ignore such issues for the sake of simplicity.

2.3. What are revenues

Revenues are defined as the income generated from the sale of products or services associated with the main operations of an organisation before any costs or expenses are deducted. Therefore, revenues are the positive income that a business gets from selling products or services, and such revenues will be used to offset the total costs incurred so that profit can be generated.

Customers might quite regularly buy goods on credit; such sales are still considered revenue even though cash may have not yet been received (hence a big difference between generating revenue and receiving a cash inflow/cash flow). For simplicity, however, we will assume that all transactions are in cash, i.e., no sales are left unpaid.

Total revenues are calculated by multiplying the number of output units sold by the price per unit (which is paid by the customer):

Total Revenues = Number of Units Sold × Price per Unit

As noted, forecasting revenues poses at least two challenges: first, we do not have a crystal ball to anticipate the number of product or service units that will be sold (we will come back to this later); and second, we also do not know what the selling price would be for the products. Let us now focus on the issue related to pricing.

Pricing is related to setting the rate at which a unit of a product (or service) will be sold. It is far more complicated than it may seem because its determination largely depends on various issues, including:

- what the customers are willing to pay for;
- the benefit that customers expect to derive from their purchase;
- the marketing strategy of the firm;
- the intrinsic characteristics and value-added by the product or service;
- the prices offered by competitors, and so on.

At this point, it is also worthwhile distinguishing between price-setting firms and price-taking firms.

A price setter is a firm that - as the name suggests - can set the price of one or several of its products to some extent in the market regardless of how the competitors have set their prices.

These will be the firms that have highly customised and differentiated products and/or are market leaders. Not all businesses can become market leaders and price setters (like Apple or Samsung).

For example, in starting up a business and no other company nearby offering similar products, the firm can be a price setter to some extent.

On the other hand, firms that must accept the price set by the market are price takers. Smaller firms operating within an industry already dominated by other players tend to be price-takers.

Even though pricing can be considered a marketing decision, the price of a product is highly influenced by many factors that the firm does not have control over.

Consequently, products and services should be sold at a rate so that the sales revenues are enough to cover all the fixed and variable costs, while at the same time, providing a satisfactory level of profit.

Therefore, the critical questions are how to assign a price to a product or service:

- Should the price be the same across all geographies and demographic characteristics of the customers?
- Should the price be based on the actual cost of production or based on what the potential buyers would be willing to pay?
- Should the price be the same throughout the whole life cycle of the product?

To simplify our discussion on this matter, we will use three pricing principles that can act as a good starting point for pricing decisions.

2.3.1. Cost-based or mark-up pricing

The price is determined by adding a profit element or mark-up on top of the cost of making the product or delivering a service:

> **Selling Price = Cost of Production + Mark-up**

An advantage of this approach is that the business will know that its costs are being covered. However, a key disadvantage is that cost-plus pricing may lead to products being priced above what the customers are willing to pay for.

Next is an example of mark-up pricing, where a business wishes to make a $50 profit on top of the cost of production per unit:

$$Selling\ Price = \$100 + \$100 \times 50\% = \$150$$

As noted, the difficulty arising from this method is related to what the mark-up percentage should be, which largely depends on the competitive prices in the market and whether the resulting price would be acceptable to customers.

In the above example, a markup of 50% was assumed arbitrarily. However, how high, or low should the markup be?

Before deciding on the markup, various factors and strategies need to be considered. These issues are discussed in the remainder of this chapter.

2.3.2. Market-based pricing

This relates to the pricing of new products, where the price is determined by the anticipation of what the customers may be willing to pay for a given product or service.

As a rule of thumb, if the business is in a highly competitive market and does not bring a lot of value or novelty to the market, customers will not be willing to pay more for the product or service. This means that the company may have to squeeze down the prices to enter the market.

This is also referred to as penetration pricing, whereby a business sets a relatively low initial entry price to attract new customers and thus penetrate the market. This strategy aims to encourage customers to switch to the new product because of its lower price.

However, one disadvantage here is that customers may not like it when the firm subsequently attempts to raise the selling price.

Conversely, if the firm is launching a new product or service for which there is little or no competition (in a somewhat monopolistic setting), it may set a high price before other competitors come into the market. This strategy is commonly known as price skimming.

Unfortunately, this strategy is difficult to maintain in the long term, mainly because competitors will ultimately launch rival products or services that will put downward pressure on the price. It may also dampen initial demand as many customers would not be able to afford it.

Further, when a product can command a high price in the market, it provides a signal to competitors that there may be plenty of opportunity for making a profit, thus encouraging more competitors to enter the market.

2.3.3. Competitor-based pricing

This approach is mostly dependent on the number of competitors in the market. If there is strong existing competition in the market, customers are faced with a wide choice of whom to buy from.

Most firms in a competitive market do not have sufficient power to be able to set prices above their competitors. Therefore, they tend to set prices that are in line with the rates charged by their direct competitors.

However, as the business objective is to maximise profits, companies should look for ways to differentiate their products from those of their competitors; for example, providing better quality, better service, faster delivery or a combination of all of these might distinguish a business from its competitors, thus enabling the firm to set a higher price.

An effective pricing strategy reflects a combination of all the above techniques. Prices are capped by what the market is willing to pay for a good or service; they should be aligned with competition after considering any differentiation that may exist, and they should always cover the costs of producing the product or service.

2.3.4. Pricing strategies for the long term

In the long term, price-setting firms can either use the cost-plus pricing approach or the target-costing approach.

As discussed earlier, the cost-plus approach involves figuring out all the costs required to produce goods and then adding a required level of profit margin on top of that to arrive at the selling price of the products.

Price-setting firms can also employ a target-costing approach where the target selling price is determined first and then the determined profit margin is deducted from the target selling price.

Whatever remains should be able to cover all the estimated costs of production; if not, costs must be brought down, or the product will have to be abandoned.

The target-costing approach is adopted at the planning and design phase before deciding whether to produce the goods. Target costing is mainly suited for non-customized products with expected sales at high volumes.

As it is vital to be aware of some of the pricing strategies that are employed in the business world, let us discuss four common pricing policies:

Promotional pricing - This strategy can take a variety of forms. It might consist of the familiar 'Save $5; was $20, now $15' sales offer.

It could also involve offering some (but not all) products at an unusually low price hoping that customers attracted by such low prices in some products would buy other regularly priced items as well.

Think of an imaginary situation where a pub lowers the price of its burgers from $5 to 'just $2.50' during certain hours.

Customers attracted by the low price of this one item might be tempted to buy other food and drink items in the pub.

Moreover, regular seasonal offers like Boxing Day or Black Friday can also be categorised as promotional pricing.

Differential pricing - This strategy involves setting different prices for the same product in various market segments.

For multiple reasons, manufacturers might decide to charge a lower price for an item ordered over the internet compared to in-store sales; technology-savvy shoppers might find a better deal online for the same product with the use of discount codes while regular shoppers may have to pay the full price even while purchasing the same item through the same medium.

For this strategy to be effective, there should be distinct market segments reacting differently to prices.

Psychological pricing - This strategy is mainly employed in consumer products where customers' purchasing habits can be expected to be influenced, to some extent, by their emotions rather than economic factors.

A conventional example of this kind of pricing is where a product may be priced at $49.99 rather than $50.00 thus giving the impression that the product is much cheaper than it is.

There can also be a situation where someone bought two pairs of jeans for the advertised price of $49.99 whereas she only needed one pair which would have cost her $34.99.

Alternatively, it could also be a case of the Buy One Get One Free offer, where a customer pays $49.99 for one pair of jeans and gets the other pair for 'free'.

Products, which usually complement each other, can also be bundled together and offered at a lower price if bought together.

Another approach to psychological pricing could be where the rate of a product is unchanged from the previous year, but the quantity is gradually reduced thus giving the false impression that the price has remained the same from the previous year.

Product-line pricing - This strategy relates to the pricing of various products within a product line. The product line, in this case, refers to multiple products that are closely related together.

For example, as an online retailer of laptops, a customer might consider laptops along with mice, or laptop bags within the same product line. If a business is selling printers, the printer itself and the ink cartridges might be within the same product line.

A strategy often employed consists of selling printers at a low price but later charging more for the ink cartridges that need to be replaced regularly.

Readers might also be familiar with situations where customers get a phone for 'free' if they pay a certain amount monthly for talk time and data.

The above discussion, of course, does not provide an exhaustive list or review of pricing methods and strategies. However, being aware of various pricing techniques and policies would be invaluable to a new business to adjust pricing strategies accordingly.

2.4. What are the margins

The margin is the difference between the selling price of a product or service and all the costs of producing it.

Hence, margins are the operational profits or losses generated before any interest has been received or paid, any depreciation of assets has been considered, or any taxes on gains have been paid.

The following table illustrates a simplified version of a profit and loss forecast statement of the NANO Company to demonstrate how this information can be analysed to evaluate the profitability of the business:

	Value
Number of units/games sold (@ $20 per unit)	50,000
Total revenues	$1,000,000
(–) Total variable costs (@ $5 per unit)	$250,000
(=) Variable margin	$750,000
(–) Total fixed costs	$200,000
(=) Operating margin	$550,000

The company sells 50,000 litres per year at a $20 selling price per litre (total revenues $1,000,000). The variable cost of producing each litre sold is $5; hence, the total variable cost equals $250,000 (= 50,000 × $5) – the variable cost is also known as the cost of sales.

Subtracting the total variable cost from the total revenues gives us the variable margin, which means that after paying for the cost of producing the inks the firm will still have $750,000 left to pay for its fixed costs. Hence,

> **Variable Margin = Total Revenues − Total Variable Costs**

Considering that the fixed costs are equal to $200,000 per year, subtracting this fixed amount from the variable margin results in a $550,000 operating margin, which in this case is a profit.

Hence,

> **Operating Margin = Variable margin − Total Fixed Costs**

However, this will not be the profit available to be distributed to the shareholders of the firm, like other costs (e.g., interest payables, taxes and depreciation) will have to be deducted before the remainder can be considered profits available to owners.

We can also calculate the variable margin per litre/unit sold, which is called the contribution margin per unit sold:

> **Contribution Margin per Unit = Selling Price per Unit − Variable Cost per Unit**

The contribution margin per unit represents the portion of sales revenue that is not consumed by producing and selling one unit and contributes towards the coverage of the company's fixed costs.

In the above example, the contribution margin per unit equals $15 which is obtained by subtracting the variable cost per unit ($5) from the selling price per unit ($20). In other words, each board game that is sold contributes $15 towards paying the fixed costs of the firm, and the resulting margin is $15 (= $20 − $5).

3. Calculating the Break-Even point

We are now in a position to calculate the Break-Even Point (BEP) of the business, which is the point at which costs and revenues are equal and there is thus neither profit nor loss. This is also known as the Cost-Volume-Profit analysis. In other words, the BEP refers to the minimum number of units of output required to be sold to have nil operating profits.

The firm will break even when it generates enough revenue to cover the overall variable and fixed costs incurred while producing and selling its products or services.

If the business sells the bare minimum units of products to meet these objectives (i.e., it reaches the BEP), it will just break even but will not earn a profit (however, and importantly, it will not make a loss either). If the business exceeds the BEP, however, it will be able to generate an operational profit.

The calculation of the BEP may be performed using two formulae. The first formula provides the result regarding the number of units of output that need to be produced (quantity) and sold to pay for the fixed costs.

The second formula calculates the BEP concerning the sales volume or revenue (typically in US dollars but can be any other currency).

We will introduce the formulae to calculate your BEP. Even though you have not at this stage started the firm and have very few or no fixed costs, you probably already have some idea of the variable costs related to the production of your product, even if in a controlled lab environment.

Nevertheless, we want you to make some assumptions as you are now testing – even though at very preliminary stages – the feasibility of your product in terms of commercialisation. Please bear in mind that you don't necessarily have to have a profitable company (as per the following analysis) to decide whether to start your business.

By no means!

Many companies that are spin-offs of academic research (particularly in the life sciences area) take years if not decades to reach profitability. No profitability in the short term should not deter investors either, so this should not be a reason for major concern.

However, we want you to understand how distant your business might be from profitability, and this is important because it will help you to source the funds needed to keep it afloat during the time it takes until it gets there. And investors understand this very well. Therefore, don't perceive the calculation of the BEP to be a barrier to moving forward, but as another tool that helps you to put things in a business and temporal perspective.

Please follow the example and try to adapt it to your product. Use the information that you have already collected about the fixed, and variable costs, etc., and replicate the calculations as if you were calculating the BEP as well.

First, BEP is calculated according to the number of units. The result is obtained by dividing the total fixed costs by the contribution margin per unit:

> **BEP (in units) = Total Fixed Costs ÷ Contribution Margin per Unit**

Returning to the example of the NANO Company:

$$BEP = \$200,000 \div \$15 = 13,333(33) \text{ units}$$

With a contribution margin of $15 per litre sold, the BEP is achieved at 13,333(33) or roughly 13,333 litres: upon the production and sale of 13,333 litres, all fixed expenses will be paid for, and the company will report a net profit or loss of $0.

This result is easy to confirm, as follows:

	Value
Number of units sold	13,333(33)
Total revenues (@ $20 per unit)	$266,666(66)
(−) Total variable costs (@ $5 per unit)	$66,66(66)
(=) Variable margin	$200,000
(−) Total fixed costs	$200,000
(=) Operating margin	**$0**

Please note that for calculation purposes we have used 13,333.33 units produced although that will be physically impossible to achieve; 13,333 is more realistic.

Alternatively, the BEP concerning sales volume can be calculated by dividing the total fixed costs by the contribution margin ratio, where the contribution margin ratio is the contribution margin per unit ($5) divided by the sale price per unit ($20), thus resulting in the BEP sales volume of $266,660.

These results suggest that we need to generate revenues of at least $266,666 for the year to break even in this business. In practical terms, these results also mean that if the firm would not able to reach the BEP (minimum sales threshold) and cover all the variable and fixed costs incurred, it will, sooner or later, run out of cash.

Nonetheless, firms may rely on obtaining additional funds to cover their needs, such as a loan or an additional investment made by the shareholders as well as acquiring new investors.

3.1. Simulating different scenarios

The advantage of the break-even analysis is that it immediately provides an accurate perspective of the minimum volume of sales that needs to be generated.

To be profitable, the firm needs to sell above the BEP; the greater the quantity in this regard, the better. Therefore, upon determining these results, one can immediately question the feasibility of achieving the BEP as well as look for ways to surpass it and generate a profit.

However, first, it is useful to ponder how firms could potentially lower their BEP, as it could benefit the cost structure of the firm and reduce its exposure to risks, namely the fluctuation of demand. To do so, and as derived from the calculation we did earlier, three variables can be changed to simulate different scenarios that will result in either an increase or decrease in the BEP:

- Fixed costs,
- Selling price per unit, and

- Variable cost per unit/cost of sales per unit.

Let us now analyse the impact on the BEP if each of these variables is changed. Going back to the NANO Company, let us first estimate the impact on the BEP by reducing the fixed costs by 20%.

The resulting fixed costs would be $160,000 (= $200,000 − 20% × $200,000).

Therefore,

$$BEP = \$160,000 \div \$15 = 10,666(67) \text{ units}$$

Hence, the BEP is reduced compared to the initial situation (13,333 units).

The rationale is that if fixed costs are reduced, the contribution margin that needs to be generated to pay for the fixed costs is also reduced, therefore putting less pressure on the objectives. Conversely, increasing the fixed costs would push the BEP up, thereby driving the firm to expand its targets.

Now let us try some simulations to see what will happen to the BEP if we maintain the initial fixed costs but increase the selling price per unit, let us say, by 20%.

The resulting new selling price per unit would be $24 (= $20 + 20% × $20).

$$BEP = \$200,000 \div (\$24 - \$5) = 10,526 \text{ units}$$

As expected, the BEP has decreased compared to the initial situation (13,333 units).

The rationale is that if the contribution margin per unit increases as a result of increasing the selling price per unit, each unit sold contributes more towards covering the fixed costs; hence, fewer units need to be sold to cover the fixed costs. Conversely, reducing the selling price would have the opposite effect and raise the BEP.

Now let us see what will happen to the BEP if we maintain the initial fixed costs and selling price per unit, but manage to reduce the variable costs per unit by 20%. The resulting variable cost per unit would be $4 (= $5 − 20% × $5).

BEP = $200,000 ÷ ($20 − $4) = 12,500 units

As expected, the BEP has decreased compared to the initial situation (13,333 units).

The rationale is that if the contribution margin per unit increases as a result of reducing the variable cost per unit, each unit sold contributes more towards covering the fixed costs; hence, fewer units need to be sold to cover the fixed costs. Conversely, increasing the variable cost per unit would have the opposite effect and raise the BEP.

The results are summarised as follows:

Simulating the impact of different variables on the BEP

Fixed costs	Selling price per unit	Variable cost per unit
Increase => BEP increases	Increase => Contribution Margin increases => BEP decreases	Increase => Contribution Margin increases => BEP increases
Decrease => BEP decreases	Decrease => Contribution Margin decreases => BEP increases	Decreases => Contribution margin increases => BEP decreases

As noted, the power of the break-even analysis is that it immediately allows us to test the feasibility of the sales objectives while also allowing us to simulate different scenarios. In doing so, we can explore whether it would be feasible to change some of the factors within the limits of what can be achieved given the constraints of resources, the business model, and strategies.

However, the analysis presented is also fundamental as it enables a better understanding of whether the sales objectives are within reach through reasonable efforts given the constraints imposed by the initial capacity of the company as well as the market size.

Now, let us expand our discussion on BEP to understand how it can be useful to test the internal capacity of a business.

3.2. Testing the operational capacity

Calculating the BEP can be very helpful in determining whether capacity adjustments must be made to the company.

As we will see, using this method will also be useful in that it may alert us to some of the pitfalls related to business planning, particularly to circumstances of under-capacity.

Let us look at the example of the NANO business which has an anticipated capacity of 100,000 litres of production per year. Can the BEP be achieved using the firm's capacity?

Yes, it can, as the BEP is 13,333 litres per year. However, this raises another important question which is whether having all that installed capacity at the firm to start with is reasonable. Ideally, the capacity should be adequate to serve the market. If the company expect to sell well above the BEP and reach around 80 to 90K litres per year, that capacity is adequate. However, if the firm expects to generate 20 or 30K litres, why pay fixed costs and potentially must spend money upfront on equipment to manufacture the product when the distance/gap to the maximum capacity is so high? This should give enough food for thought in terms of planning the capacity of a firm when starting a business.

Therefore, decisions would have to be made about how to make this economically feasible. We assume that, in principle, there would not be much margin of manoeuvre to change either the selling price which is capped by the competition, or the variable costs per litre of ink produced.

The most likely options at this stage would be to attempt to manage the fixed costs and potentially plan of starting with a smaller capacity to reduce any business risks from the outset. On the other hand, the BEP formula can also help you to detect potential problems ahead if you have less capacity than you need to reach the BEP.

This approach deals with the identification of the internal capacity of the business regarding how many units of product or service could be produced given a certain level of initial capacity to start.

The capacity can be expanded or reduced over time but, as noted previously, higher capacity could mean higher fixed costs.

Therefore, it is advisable to consider setting up a reasonable capacity that minimises fixed costs and consider the possibility to scale it up later when the market demand grows.

A good strategy at the market-entry stage when firms are unsure of how the market will react would be to consider outsourcing the production (entirely or partially) to other firms.

In doing so the business would probably end up paying more for the production which would increase its variable costs, however, the fixed costs structure would be kept at minimum levels, therefore reducing the risks.

However, this is a strategic and challenging decision to be made as it is not always possible to outsource the production to third parties, either because none can provide the same standards of quality, the price (and variable costs) may be too high to bear; or just because the firm does not trust another partner to handover knowledge and expertise which may be critical for the business.

3.3. A temporal perspective for the BEP

The BEP can also assist you in identifying when in the year you will reach that threshold. One can assume the sales volume per year. In the first example of the NANO Company, the sales volume per year was 50K litres of paint, which is far above the BEP.

If the firm sells on average the same quantity each quarter, this means that the firm sells 12,500 litres per quarter. Looking at the BEP, which is 13,333 litres, this means that soon after the first quarter of sales the firm will be entering the "profit zone". Happy days ahead for the rest of the year!

3.4. Defining profitability objectives

Until now, we have used break-even analysis to allow us to answer a fundamental question: How many units of product or service need to be sold to break even and make a nil profit?

However, the nature of any business activity is to generate a profit and so this raises another critical question: What sales volume needs to be achieved to make the business profitable?

To illustrate this, a slight modification can be made to the existing formula as follows:

> **BEP (in units) = (Total Fixed Costs + Profit) ÷ Contribution Margin**

The result will give us the excess sales (in units) that must be made to achieve this objective.

Going back to the NANO Company, the initial BEP was estimated as being achieved by selling 13,333 litres in a year. However, this means a nil profit after the operating costs have been accounted for.

Now, let us assume that the management had the objective of achieving a gross profit of $500,000 for the first year of trade.

One way to estimate how this would impact the sales objectives is by adding this required profit amount to the fixed costs and recalculating the BEP:

$$BEP = (\$500{,}000 + \$200{,}000) \div \$15 = 46{,}666(66) \text{ units}$$

Hence, the difference between this and the previous BEP would be an additional 33,333 litres that need to be sold to achieve that profit for the year.

3.5. Further examples

This section aims to provide further examples and clarifications on how the break-even analysis can be used in planning a start-up business. Specifically, two examples are discussed to demonstrate the applicability of the break-even analysis in two different businesses: service-oriented business and product-related business.

3.5.1. Example 1 - Counselling practice

This example specifically refers to counselling practice, but it could also be applied to any freelance practice in the health sector, or other sectors such as accounting, web design or computer programming.

Therefore, the example provided should be used as a guideline that can be easily adopted by anyone starting a similar venture.

The business will have only one employee, the founder. An office will be rented to attend to customers and conduct the therapy sessions.

The therapy sessions will be carried out on the premises so there would be no additional travelling to meet customers in other locations. The unit of output is a one-hour session of therapy.

First, let us identify the fixed costs relating to establishing such a practice. Whenever costs are paid on an annual basis (such as insurance, professional membership fees, etc.), we divide the figure by 12 to allow for a monthly estimation.

Fixed costs	Monthly value
Accounting and legal fees	$65
Insurances	$20
Sales and marketing	$50
Rent of the premises	$500
Office supplies	$45
Salaries and wages	$2,280
Total	**$2,960**

To estimate the variable costs, we need to identify the costs that could be directly connected to each one-hour session. If providing this service entails travelling to visit a customer, then the associated costs should be considered variable costs.

In this example, let us assume that the direct variable costs associated with a one-hour therapy session would be as follows:

Variable costs	Per unit
Printing of materials to support the therapy	$1
Essential oils needed for the treatment	$2
Total	**$3**

The price charged by the therapist per hour is $50. To calculate the BEP, we will use the formulas previously described, as follows:

Contribution Margin = Selling Price per Unit − Variable Costs per Unit

Hence,

Contribution Margin = $50 − $3 = $47

And to determine the BEP:

BEP = Total Fixed Costs ÷ Contribution Margin

Hence,

BEP = $2,960 ÷ $47 = 62.98 sessions per month (one hour each)

To facilitate the analysis, the figure is rounded up to the nearest integer value, namely 63 sessions.

The result means that to pay for the fixed costs, the counsellor needs to fill 63 one-hour sessions, which will turn over approximately $3,150 per month (=63×$50).

From an operational perspective, 63 sessions per month would represent an average of 15.75 sessions per week (considering four weeks per calendar month) and 3.15 sessions per day (assuming five working days per week), which is feasible for such a business in its early stages.

We will discuss the applicability of the break-even analysis for an online retailer in the following section.

3.5.2. Example 2 - Online retailer

This example relates explicitly to the establishment of an online company that sells fashion jewellery but it could also be applied to any practice that trades goods either online or in a retail shop.

Therefore, the example provided should be used as a guideline that can help with the implementation of a methodology that can be easily used by anyone involved in a similar venture.

In this example, the self-employed founder will be the only employee. The unit of output is one order which includes one item of jewellery (e.g. earrings, bracelet, necklace, or ring).

The company plans to offer a catalogue of approximately 500 different items of jewellery and an average stock of 20 units of each, meaning that the overall stock will be around 10,000 units.

The stock is imported to the UK from China. The cost range including taxes is between $1 and $2 per item, with an average price of $1.50 per item. The pieces are stocked in the UK and dispatched to customers internationally.

One small warehouse will be rented to stock and prepare the dispatching of orders. The company will replenish its stock as appropriate considering the sales accomplished.

The selling price is established by applying a 700% markup to the purchase price, meaning that on average the selling price per item will be $10.5 (=$1.50×7), excluding postage.

This price is within the range that is accepted in the market for similar goods sold online in the UK.

For simplification purposes, no taxes such as VAT will be considered in this example.

All the sales are generated online through the company's website as well as by using third-party e-commerce platforms such as eBay and Amazon.

It is estimated that, in the beginning, 99% of the sales will be generated through these third channels, which charge an average of 20% commission (applied to the selling price) on every purchase.

It is also estimated that 90% of the sales will be generated in the UK and only 10% overseas.

First, let us identify the fixed costs relating to the establishment of such a business. As previously mentioned, whenever costs are paid on an annual basis, we divide the figure by 12 to allow for a monthly estimation.

Fixed costs	Monthly value
Rent of the premises	$500
Office supplies	$60
Insurances	$20
Sales and marketing	$50
Accounting and legal fees	$65
Salaries and wages	$2,230
Total	**$2,925**

To estimate the variable costs per unit, we now need to identify the direct costs of each different item. For break-even analysis, this would be very time-consuming, and it would not bring much value to a high-level approach which is the one we intend to use in this methodology.

The assumption that will be applied to this example is to consider the average costs per item as being $1.50 and the average selling price per unit to be $10.50. Therefore, the average cost per item would be 14.29% (=$1.5÷$10.5) of the selling price.

In this example, let us assume that the direct variable costs associated with one sale would be as follows:

Variable costs	Per unit
Purchase cost per item	$1.50
Commission per sale (20% of the selling price)	$2.10
Packaging per item sold	$1.20
Postage per item sold	$0.80
Total	$5.60

To calculate the BEP, we will use the formulas previously described, as follows:

Contribution Margin = Selling Price per Unit – Variable Costs per Unit

Hence,

Contribution Margin = $10.50 – $5.60 = $4.90

And considering that

BEP (in units) = Total Fixed Costs ÷ Contribution Margin

Hence,

BEP = $2,925 ÷ $4.90 = 596.94 items per month

To facilitate our analysis, we will round the figure to the nearest integer value, namely 597 items. From an operational perspective, 597 items per month would represent an average of 19.9 (or 20) items per day (assuming 30 days/month on average). Achieving this result would probably not be very feasible in the beginning, but it is within what is expected to be achievable in the medium term as the company gains an online presence and enhances its reputation.

4. Building a financial model (Budget, P&L, and Cash flow statements)

In the previous section, we focussed mainly on the break-even analysis which provides clear operational targets to be achieved to avoid losses for a business.

However, a company also needs detailed plans to coordinate different functions (like production, marketing, sales, or recruitment) within the business so that the operation is smooth and profitable.

Implementing a budgeting process can be of help in the planning process, and this is what will be discussed in this chapter.

The word budget is heard on numerous occasions:

- the government talks about the budget almost every year which invariably leads to arguments and counterarguments among politicians and economists;
- the local authority might declare that they cannot do the repairs on the road due to a lack of budget;
- consumers might be complaining that they cannot buy that new gadget because it is not within their budget.

A budget in all these contexts is related to the expected costs and revenues/income for a given period.

However, budgeting is not just about forecasting costs; it is also about projecting various other aspects of business-like marketing, recruitment, production volume, and so on.

Therefore, it helps not just with planning but can also be useful for controlling operations and evaluating performance, among other things.

But why do businesses need a budget? Let us go back to the example of GAME Company with anticipated sales of 40,000 games in December. Imagine the disruption to the operation of the business running out of the required materials to produce the games just before that peak month.

Alternatively, imagine that the necessary materials are there but not enough workforce to package the games during the period of high demand!

These are some of the situations a business should try to avoid, by careful planning ahead.

There are different types of budgets like production budgets, sales budgets, cash budgets, and so on.

With so many different budgets, which budget is the better one to start with first?

The budget begins with the critical factor which is generally the revenues (i.e. the money that the business plans to generate by selling products or services).

Hence, it is the Revenues or Sales Budget that needs to be prepared first and then other budgets like material purchase budget, and advertising budget can follow, based on the sales budget.

4.1. Master budget

The master budget comprises different sub-budgets which are interlinked, and altogether allow a better understanding of the various inputs that the firm needs to mobilise in advance and to meet the sales objectives.

Let us start with forecasting the sales for the GAME Company.

Based on the previous findings, the GAME Company expects to attain a 10% market share during the first year, therefore, being able to sell in the region of 50,000 units.

Accordingly, they have prepared an annual budget which can be broken down into four quarters. We will work on the budget for the last quarter of the year, ending on the 31st of December 201X.

	Oct	Nov	Dec
Expected Sales (in units)	2,000	3,000	10,000

For simplicity, we assume that the selling price per unit will remain at $20 for the foreseeable future; this allows us to prepare a sales budget in monetary terms easily.

We multiply each month's expected sales in units with the expected sales price ($20) to come up with the Sales Budget as follows:

	Oct	Nov	Dec
Expected sales (in units)	2,000	3,000	10,000
Selling price per unit ($)	$20	$20	$20
Expected sales ($)	$40,000	$60,000	$200,000

To ensure smooth supply to the customers and to avoid missing sales targets due to insufficient stock, the company might decide to hold about 20% of the following month's sales as a reserve.

This information allows us to calculate the monthly Production Budget, as follows:

	Oct	Nov	Dec
Expected sales (in units)	2,000	3,000	10,000
(+) Required closing stock (in units)	600	2,000	0
(=) Total stock needs	2,600	5,000	10,000
(–) Opening stock	100	600	2,000
(=) Production units	2,500	4,400	8,000

The above budget shows that, for October, 2,500 units of products need to be produced (even though the expected sales are only 2,000 units).

This is because, on top of the required units of 2,000 for October, an additional 600 units are needed (20% of November's requirement of 3,000) as a safety reserve for the following month.

The same applies to November and December. We will assume that the closing stock of December is nil as after the peak season (Christmas) the sales are expected to drop sharply for the following months; we will also assume that the opening balance for October (i.e. closing balance for September) is 100.

However, there are also 100 stock units in the opening balance from September (the closing balance for September is the opening balance for October).

Hence, there is a need to produce 2,500 units (=2,000+600−100) in September. The same applies to November and December.

A natural progression from this point forward would be to estimate the direct materials to purchase in the future to keep up with the production.

Let us assume that the firm needs 1.2 Kg of materials (which would include all materials including plastics, cardboard, cards, and packaging) to produce one unit of the final product ready for delivery.

To avoid any disruption in supplies, let us consider that the firm keeps 20% of the following month's production requirement in stock.

For October, we will assume that the opening balance (i.e. closing balance from September) is 370 Kg.

We can now prepare a material Purchase Budget for the quarter.

	Oct	Nov	Dec
Production units	2,500	4,400	8,000
Materials needed (Kg)	3,000	5,280	9,600
(+) Required closing stock (Kg)	1,056	1,920	0
(=) Total materials needed (Kg)	4,056	7,200	9,600
(−) Opening stock (Kg)	370	1,056	1,920
(=) Materials purchase (Kg)	3,686	6,144	7,680

Now the business has a rough idea of how much materials it needs to buy every month. For example, during November, the firm needs to buy 6,144 Kg of materials.

In real life, it will also have a fair idea of how much each Kg of materials is going to cost. To keep things simple, let us assume that each Kg of materials cost $2.20.

This allows us to figure out the amount of money that would be needed to buy these materials for each of the coming months. For October, the amount of money required to purchase the necessary materials would be $8,109 (=3,686×$2.20), and so on for other months.

	Oct	Nov	Dec
Materials purchase (Kg)	3,686	6,144	7,680
Materials purchase ($)	8,109	13,517	16,896

Taking a step further, now let us assume that the direct labour needed to prepare one board game is six minutes.

This is to say that one individual would have to work for six minutes (0.1 hours) to make one board ready for selling.

If the semi-skilled worker needs to be paid $12 per hour, it is possible to figure out how many labour hours would be needed for production purposes and the cost of such labour hours.

This can be done using the Direct Labour Budget as shown next:

	Oct	Nov	Dec
Production units	2,500	4,400	8,000
Required Labour Hours	250	440	800
Direct Labour Cost ($)	3,000	5,280	9,600

Apart from the money needed for the purchase of materials (as worked out in one of the earlier tables), this new information allows us to estimate the additional amount of money needed each month to pay direct wages.

The derived number of labour hours enables us to figure out roughly how many individuals need to be hired during each of the above months.

For instance, if one individual works 150 hours per month, the number of individuals necessary for October is 2 (=250÷150).

Similarly, for November, approximately three individuals would be needed and for December five individuals for direct production.

Possessing this information would enable the business owner to estimate the recruitment and training needs.

So far, we have taken into account direct costs (i.e. direct materials and direct labour). Let us now account for indirect materials and indirect labour as well.

Let us assume that the variable manufacturing overhead is $0.50 (50 pence) per unit produced and the fixed manufacturing overhead is $1,800 per month. This fixed manufacturing overhead would be incurred regardless of the number of products produced (and sold).

Therefore, the Manufacturing Overhead Budget would look like this:

	Oct	Nov	Dec
Production units	2,500	4,400	8,000
Variable manufacturing overhead ($0.5)	1,250	2,200	4,000
(+) Fixed manufacturing overhead ($)	1,800	1,800	1,800
(=) Total manufacturing overheads ($)	3,050	4,000	5,800

We will add one more category of costs to our budget now: selling and administrative. This cost will be based on the sales figure rather than the production units.

If we assume a selling cost of $2.50 per unit sold (for postage and delivery) along with a fixed selling and admin cost of $700 a month to cover other rubrics, we can easily make the Administrative Budget as follows:

	Oct	Nov	Dec
Sales units	2,000	3,000	10,000
Variable selling & admin ($)	5,000	7,500	25,000
(+) Fixed selling & admin ($)	700	700	700
(=) Total selling & admin ($)	5,700	8,200	25,700

The above table illustrates that the total selling and administration expenses for October will be $5,700. Similar estimates are shown for November and December thereby giving the business owners opportunity to plan accordingly.

4.2. Cash-based budgeting

A cash budget details a company's cash inflow (money received) and cash outflow (money paid out) during a specified period, such as a month, quarter, or year. Its purpose is to provide the status of the company's cash position at any point in time, and it is used to assess whether the business has sufficient money to operate.

Companies use sales forecasts to create a cash budget, along with assumptions about mandatory spending.

If a company does not have enough money to operate either in the long term or short term, it must raise more capital by issuing stock or by taking on debt.

In the case of a start-up or expanding a business, a cash-based budget is of utmost relevance for estimating the needs of liquidity.

This is because the firm will not start generating money immediately as it needs to enter the market, promote its offer before having customers, and make sales.

Hence, the firm needs to have a clear idea about operating cash flow, which is a measure of the amount of money generated by a company's normal business operations.

Operating cash flow indicates whether a company can make sufficient positive money flow to maintain and grow its operations; or if it may require external financing for business expansion.

Operating cash flows concentrate on cash inflows and outflows related to the firm's principal business activities, such as selling (cash in) and purchasing inventory, providing services, and paying salaries (cash out).

Any investing and financing transactions (e.g. interest on a loan) are excluded from operating cash flows and reported separately, such as borrowing money or making capital expenditures. However, we will address these issues later.

Using the tables that we have prepared so far in the previous section, we are in a position to prepare a cash budget; i.e. a budget that tells us about the cash position of the business.

An important reminder is that this is not a profit/loss account (which we will deal with later).

Assuming that the opening cash balance for October was -$20,000 (i.e. $20,000 into an overdraft), the cash budget would look as follows:

	Oct	Nov	Dec
Opening balance	-$20,000	$141	$29,144
Sales	$40,000	$60,000	$200,000
(−) Less:			
Materials Purchase	$8,109	$13,517	$16,896
Direct Labour	$3,000	$5,280	$9,600
Variable manufacturing overhead	$1,250	$2,200	$4,000
Fixed manufacturing overhead	$1,800	$1,800	$1,800
Selling and admin	$5,700	$8,200	$25,700
(=) Closing balance	$141	$29,144	$171,148

In the above table, the cash inflows and outflows for each month are used to determine the month's ending balance, which is the beginning balance for the following month.

This process allows the company to forecast its cash needs throughout the year.

The above projection shows that the business will have more cash available throughout the quarter. So far, we have made the predictions in the simplest of settings without considering so many complexities that one may have to deal with in real life.

For example:

- Shall we get the full amount of sales revenue in cash?
- Alternatively, how much of that would turn into irrecoverable debt?

- How long will the buyers take to pay the company for the goods supplied?

Let us incorporate the effect of the delay in collecting the cash generated by sales in the previous cash-based budget.

For this purpose, the company forecasts that 80% of the receipts will be collected in the same month as the sale and the other 20% received one month after the sale.

All the other costs are expected to be incurred in the respective month.

	Oct	Nov	Dec
Opening balance	-$20,000	-$2,859	$22,144
(+) Payment Collection	$37,000	$56,000	$172,000
(=) Cash inflows	$17,000	$53,141	$194,144
(−) Variable costs	$17,359	$28,497	$55,496
(−) Fixed costs	$2,500	$2,500	$2,500
(=) Cash outflows	$19,859	$30,997	$57,996
Closing balance (inflows−outflows)	-$2,859	$22,144	$136,148

In this example, the GAME Company computes the cash inflows by adding the initial cash position (October) to the receivables collected during that month (80% of the sales made), plus the receivables collected from the transactions made in September (20%) which we assume are $5,000.

In this month, as the cash outflows will total $19,859, the company will have a negative cash balance of $2,859 at the end of the month.

This is assumed to be covered by a bank overdraft allowance that the company has previously negotiated, and which will incur charges. To simplify the discussion, we will not include these overdraft charges in our analysis.

This negative cash balance will be the initial cash position in October. To compute the cash inflows during that month, the negative cash position will be added to the sales collected that month.

In November, the company will receive in cash $48,000 (=$60,000×80%) plus 20% of the sales generated in October which were not collected in the previous month and represent $8,000 (=$40,000×20%), therefore, totalling $56,000.

Hence, the cash inflows will be -$2,859+$56,000=$53,141. Note that the remaining 20% of the sales made in November will only be collected in December.

The cash outflows in November will be $30,997, which will be subtracted from the inflows resulting in a positive cash balance of $22,144 in that month.

Using the same methodology for December, the company will have a positive cash balance of $136,148.

As noted, there is a big difference at the end of the year cash position of the firm according to this example, which is more realistic, as compared to the previous case ($171,148) which did not take into consideration the delay in collecting money from sales.

In practical terms, the firm could also delay its payments to the suppliers for some time, which could significantly ease its cash position.

Depending on the nature of the business, companies need to have cash in advance that will allow them to pay for the operational costs before they can generate any revenues. Such a cash balance should be enough to pay for operational expenses and keep the business afloat on its own.

4.2.1. Capital and Operating expenditures

Furthermore, some companies need to spend money upfront to set up the adequate infrastructure and resources that are required in advance of starting the business.

The upfront costs that need to be made only once to establish a business properly are commonly referred to as capital expenditures (or CAPEX).

Therefore, capital expenditures are the funds that a business uses to purchase primary physical goods or services to start or expand the company's abilities to generate profits. They are expected to provide utility to a business for more than one year.

Examples of capital expenditures:
- Buildings and Land
- Office equipment
- Machinery and Vehicles
- Software
- Intangible assets such as patents

To establish a cash budget, the company needs to be able to anticipate the CAPEX and forecast the sales as well as the fixed and variable costs that comprise the operating expenditures (or OPEX).

An operating cost is incurred to buy a business through its normal operations. These costs generally include the same categories of costs, which we have previously discussed when introducing fixed and variable costs.

As operational costs make up the bulk of a company's regular spending, the management will examine ways of lowering them without causing a critical drop in quality or production output.

Let us consider an extended version of the previous example in which the GAME Company had to make an upfront investment of $50,000 in October to market a new game that would be released during the Christmas season.

Considering this CAPEX in the budget helps in understanding when the business will make enough cash to be able to pay back the initial investment and start generating a profit.

The significance of adding the CAPEX investment to the previous model is that it clearly shows whether the business can generate enough cash flow to pay for the upfront costs on top of being able to pay for the operational costs, and most importantly when the cash flows will become positive.

To do this, we can include the initial investment as a cash outflow in September and run the model with this new element:

	Oct	Nov	Dec
Opening balance	-$20,000	-$52,859	-$27,856
(+) CAPEX	-$50,000	$0	$0
(+) Revenues	$37,000	$56,000	$172,000
(=) Cash inflows	-$33,000	$3,141	$144,144
(−) Variable costs	$17,359	$28,497	$55,496
(−) Fixed costs	$2,500	$2,500	$2,500
(=) Cash outflows	$19,859	$30,997	$57,996
Closing balance (inflows−outflows)	-$52,859	-$27,856	$86,148

As shown, although the cash position at the end of the year was still favourable, the company accumulated negative cash balances in October and November, until it finally had a positive cash flow in December.

4.3. Profit and Loss statement

A Profit and Loss (P&L) statement is a summary statement exhibiting the revenues, costs, and resulting profit (or loss) during a specific period, usually a fiscal quarter or year.

These records provide information about a company's ability - or lack thereof - to generate profit by increasing revenue, reducing costs, or both.

The P&L statement is also referred to as the statement of profit and loss, income statement, statement of comprehensive income, statement of financial results, and income and expense statement.

The P&L statement follows a general form, beginning with an entry for revenues, known as the top line, and subtracts the costs of doing business, including the cost of goods sold operating costs, taxes, interests, and depreciation.

After deducting all these costs, what remains is the net income, known as the profit (also referred to as the bottom line or earnings).

In this case, we will establish a P&L budget using the assumptions of the previous examples to help in clarifying how this table is made and the main differences between the P&L and cash-based budget. This will be helpful to explore the concept of profitability further.

The P&L statement can be used to measure the past performance of a company as well as to make a budget. The main difference, when compared to the cash-based budget, is that P&L ignores when actual cash inflows and cash outflows occur, but only considers the underlying activities that will lead to the generation of such cash flows.

For example, a company making a sale does not mean that it always collects the money after the transaction has been made. It is a standard business practice, particularly between companies, that the seller issues an invoice that is sent to the buyer, who should pay it within an agreed period.

When such invoices are sent out but are yet to be paid, they are referred to as accounts receivables for the firm.

It may be reasonable for such receivables to remain outstanding for a few weeks or even months. In P&L statements, such sales are still included even though the actual money may not have been received by the firm; whereas, in a cash budget, the sales on credit will be ignored because the firm has received no cash for such a credit sale.

Hence from the perspective of P&L analyses, the revenue generated by the sale should be considered in the P&L statement in the same accounting period (e.g. quarter or year) that the sale was made regardless of whether the transaction was on cash or credit; but from the perspective of the cash-based budget, only actual receipts (cash inflow) during the accounting period are considered regardless of when the transaction was made.

The same applies to costs. As companies buy from third parties not only resources such as goods and raw materials but also other services (such as utilities) that they need to support their business activities, they receive invoices from the suppliers that need to be paid.

The firm itself may delay making such payments by weeks or even months for various reasons. Monies owed to others by the firm are generally referred to as account payables, and such payables are still subtracted from the P&L statement to arrive at the profit figure.

The invoices are recorded in the month in which the costs were made (or resources consumed).

However, they are recorded in the cash-based budget only when the costs are paid off by the firm (cash outflow).

To make this understandable here is how a P&L statement could be made using the same information as the previous example:

	Oct	Nov	Dec	Total
Revenues	$37,000	$56,000	$172,000	$265,000
(–) Costs of goods sold	$14,159	$22,797	$32,296	$69,252
(=) Gross profit	$22,841	$33,203	$139,704	$195,748
(–) Other costs	$5,700	$8,200	$25,700	$39,600
(=) Net profit	$17,141	$25,003	$114,004	$156,148

As this is not a cash budget, the initial line is suppressed (initial cash position), for simplification purposes we will assume that the production costs are named as the costs of goods sold.

Subtracting the cost of goods sold from the revenues, we get the gross profit.

After that, we deduct the other fixed and variable costs that are not directly related to the production of the goods (depreciation, selling and admin as well as interests) and obtain the net profit.

As noted, at the end of the quarter, the accumulated net profit for the company is $156,148, which is obtained by adding up the net profits for all the months within the accounting period up to that point.

On the other hand, the cash balance at December-end stands at $86,148 only.

In practical terms, both these approaches (cash-based budget and P&L) complement each other when analysing the feasibility of a business, and therefore should be used not only to make forecasts but also to measure the performance of the firm against the objectives that were initially envisaged.

Another difference between P&L and cash budget is that the P&L statement also considers some non-cash accounting items such as depreciation. Depreciation is considered a cost but actual cash outflows do not occur for depreciation.

For example, a van purchased last year for $10,000 might be worth $8,000 this year and, as such, the depreciation cost for the van for the year would be $2,000; but this money is not paid out to anyone and hence is not an actual cash outflow for the year. However, this discussion is beyond the scope of the current book.

4.4. Determining the funding needs for the business

Now we are in a better position to ascertain the funding needs for your business at the startup stage. As you can imagine, very few businesses will start trading and generating revenues straight away.

It can take a long time (months or even years) until the first sales kick in, and therefore, the business must have alternative means to set up its operation and cope with no revenues. And this is why it is so important to anticipate the revenues (or no revenues) and particularly the upfront investments that you may need to make (CAPEX) as well as the operating costs of running the business (OPEX) so that you can ascertain how much cash the business will need until it becomes self-sufficient.

In this sense, using the information provided in budgets (and particularly the cash-based budget) is a great help to be better prepared when someone asks you the following question:

How much money do you need for your business and why?

For startup businesses, it is usually considered the burn rate of cash is an indicator of how much funds will have to be raised in anticipation, to allow the firm to survive the first months/years until sales start and grow.

The burn rate in financial terms means all the fixed and variable costs added for the whole year, so you can figure out the yearly burn rate or the monthly burn rate. Now, this raises a concern for entrepreneurs about the sources of funds that can be used. As you may guess, a startup business has no track record which makes it difficult to obtain credit (loan) from a lender, such as a bank.

In the exceptional cases that that is possible, you may end up with high-interest rates, which will put too much pressure on your business, as you won't be able to generate enough revenues to cover the operating costs, not to speak the financial costs of the business.

A good way to overcome this – but again very difficult – would be to negotiate with the lender a period during which you would not have to pay back interest nor repay the principal (capital), to give you more peace of mind to focus on the growth of the business. But in the end, credit is not a good option nor easy to obtain for startups.

The other way around this will be applying for grants that are frequently available by governmental and private funds, usually related to specific sectors of activity or industries, as well as grants available for entrepreneurs who create their workplace, for example.

Worth taking a look and seeing whether you may qualify for any of these mechanisms, as they vary significantly by country, but these mechanisms mean usually free cash without the need for any repayment. But of course, you are expected to report o the grant provider to justify how you are using the grant money, and whether or not specific outcomes that had been agreed on are being met, etc.

Another alternative for startups is to raise funds by selling a part of the equity of the firm, and for that, the entrepreneurs must be able to convince potential investors that their project is worth the risks. Equity investors can be anyone interested in buying a stake in your business, such as family or friends, but they can also be business angels (who do this regularly across many businesses), or venture capital funds.

The main difference between business angels and venture capitalists is that the angels tend to invest small amounts of cash in a business – frequently in the region of $25 to $200, and plan to sell in shorter terms to a bigger investor such as a VC which usually invests tickets above $500K. Of course, you may also need to captivate more than one investor such as a group of business angels with smaller tickets each that pledge the amount that you need to raise.

Equity investors buy a share of the equity in the firm and become its shareholders with the same rights as you and other founders may have.

As such, they will not expect the firm to pay back the money they had invested, but of course, they expect to receive it as a dividend, which means that they expect to receive every year (once the firm becomes profitable) a percentage of the profits that have been agreed to be distributed by the shareholders by the firm (more on this in the section about the legal structures of businesses in the UK).

Another way of cashing in their investment and making a profit from a shareholders standpoint – and this applies to you as well as to any other shareholders in your business – is by selling the percentage of equity that you have in the business either partially or totally, to another investor who is willing to buy it.

Raising cash from investors poses an important question, which is related to the valuation of your business. For example, let's say that you may need to raise $100K to be able to make the upfront investments (CAPEX) and run the business operations (OPEX) for the first year, as you expect to start generating revenues towards the first year of trade, and profits only during the second year of trade.

Now let's assume that you will pitch yourself and your business project to some investors and will be asking for $100K, but how much percentage of your business you will be willing to give away?

If, for example, you plan to sell 10% of the business, that implies a valuation of $100K÷10% = $1,000,000. That's it, one million USD! But how to convince an investor to invest $100K in a business and value it at $1,000,000 without the business existing or without a good track record in the first place?

That is why it is good to prepare yourself very well and to justify your ideas, plans and of course the rationale for the amount. The next chapter includes some important information that you may want to consider for being able to look at your business from the perspective of an investor and better understand how they make their decisions.

You can, of course, reduce the valuation to be more convincing and potentially have better chances of it working out. Let's say that you plan to raise the $100K but in return for 40% of the equity in the business, thus, implying a valuation of $250,000. Easier?

In the end, the process of raising funds from investors is always a negotiation so be prepared to be flexible and to also factor into your decisions the value that the investors can bring into your business beyond the cash, such as their expertise, mentoring and networks!

In addition to the previous, we would also like to discuss other alternative sources of funding for a business that may be overlooked by entrepreneurs, namely crowdsourcing.

Crowdsourcing online platforms work very well and can be explored as a means to raise equity from investors in a more convenient way in the sense that you don't have to pitch the project individually to each of them, but you do it to the platform which will market the project for you within its audience (known as crowdfunding). Numerous platforms operate on this front, and of course, they will all charge a fixed commission or variable fee in case you manage to raise the funds.

Crowdfunding platforms also operate loan-based funds which means that they can potentially get you a better deal interest-wise compared to the more traditional lenders (such as banks).

However, our thoughts about bringing in here crowdsourcing as an option, are motivated by how some crowdsourcing platforms operate (non-related to equity nor loans), whereby you can do a presell of a product to a large crowd, without having the product produced in large quantities in the first place.

You pitch to the crowd a prototype of a product, and if they are willing to buy it from you, you will use the funds to use in the manufacturing process, which otherwise you could not potentially fund. This approach has three main advantages compared to all the rest. First and foremost, you are selling a product that can be just a prototype now when you start the campaign.

Second, and perhaps most importantly, once the campaign is successful and you deliver the products, you will be able to get feedback from literally hundreds or even thousands of potential buyers who will use and test the first version of your product and will provide you with greater insights about its features, design, and benefits, etc., that you can use to improve and perfect future versions of the product.

Third, you will be connecting your product and business to a wide audience and creating a network of followers and prescribers of your product to others, thus increasing the prospects of greater market penetration in the short term, whilst also significantly increasing the brand awareness about your product and business.

5. Financial KPIs: Payback, IRR, NPV

So, let us now imagine that we have thought about our potential business; and have taken steps to estimate the initial investment needed, the yearly sales, various costs, and even profit!

Now, the question we may want to ask is this:

Can the profit that we expect to earn from the business be reasonable compensation for the risk that we are taking (by investing our wealth)?

Let us suppose that we have $30,000 to invest in a business. The compensation that we want for that investment would depend on the level of risk that the business possesses.

If the reward is adequate, we would be happy to invest; otherwise, we would not want to invest. This is as simple as this!

However, how do we define adequate compensation?

Going back to the example of our $30,000, we can invest that money in a virtually risk-free investment like a UK government bond and the yearly return (interest) can be expected to be pitiful. We would probably get an annual interest of 1% (or $300).

Though this level of return can be considered minimal, we are sure to get that return, and our investment will never be lost because the UK government can be reasonably expected to pay back the money!

In that sense, the investment is secure, but the return (interest) is probably not that good.

So, if we invest our money in a business, which is going to be riskier compared to the previous scenario and expect to get a return of 1% per year, it is no good because we could earn that much (1%) by taking no risk at all.

Since we are putting our money on the line by investing, we would need an adequate award to compensate for that extra risk being undertaken.

Though figuring out the required rate of return for a rational investor is beyond the scope of this book, we will assume that 15% (per year) is the appropriate compensation that would make us happy for the business risk undertaken.

With this information, we can now formally proceed towards doing calculations on whether a business should be conducted from a purely monetary and risk perspective.

Now suppose that we have invested $30,000 into a business, and the net profit we can expect at the end of the 1st 2nd and the 3rd year is $9,000, $13,000, and $15,000 respectively.

To keep things simple, let us also assume that the machinery we bought for this business will be obsolete by the end of the 3rd year which means we will have to cough up another $25,000 if we want to continue with the activity. Based on the riskiness of the business and the possibility that we could lose our investment; we want a 15% return per year as compensation for the risk we are taking. Is the business worth investing in?

From a naive perspective, it might seem like a worthwhile investment because we are going to get back a total of $37,000 (=$9,000+$13,000+$15,000), which is more than our initial investment of $30,000. However, we have not considered the time value of money which says that $1 today is worth more than $1 tomorrow. This is because we are expected to earn an interest in our capital.

To illustrate further, another investment option we have is to put the money in the Dodgy Bank which is offering a fixed rate of interest of 15% per year on a three-year deposit, interest paid annually, and the capital returned at maturity.

In essence, by depositing the money in this bank, our $30,000 today should be worth $34,500 next year, by adding the initial deposit to $4,500 of interest paid by the bank (=$30,000×15%); which is to say that $30,000 today is worth $34,500 one year from now, or, to put it the other way around, $34,500 one year from now is equal to $30,000 currently (at that specific level of risk).

Now let us look at the pay-outs from the next options:

	Today	Year 1	Year 2	Year 3
New Business Project				
Cash Flows	-$30,000	$9,000	$13,000	$15,000
Present value today of the future cash flows	-$30,000	$7,826	$9,830	$9,863
Net present value	-$2,481			
Dodgy Bank				
Cash Flows	-$30,000	$4,500	$4,500	$34,500
Present value today of the future cash flows	-$30,000	$3,913	$3,403	$22,684
Net present value	$0			

The $9,000 expected one year from now in our proposed investment is worth only $7,826 now!

To put it differently, if we deposit $7,826 now at 15% interest in a bank having a similar level of risk, we will get $9,000 back after one year [=$7,826+$1,174 interest (=$7,826×15%)].

The following simple formula can give an easier way of finding the present value of any amount of money:

Net Present Value = Future Value ÷ (1 + required rate) period

where the period is the number of periods (in this case years) after which the cash inflow is expected.

So, for the first cash inflows from the New Project,

Net Present Value = $9,000 ÷ (1 + 15%)1 = $7,826

Similarly, for the second cash inflow,

$$\textit{Net Present Value} = \$13{,}000 \div (1 + 15\%)^2 = \$9{,}830$$

and so on.

If we add all the present values of the expected cash flows and take away the initial investment, we are left with a Net Present Value of -$2,481 (note the negative sign) in the first example.

This is to say that we will be worse off by $2,481 if we invest in that project because the present value of all the future cash flows is less than what we are spending now on that project.

On the other hand, our investment in the bank would yield $4,500 each year in the form of interest, and we will also get our initial deposit of $30,000 at the end of three years (hence the final payment of $34,500).

Since our required rate of return was 15% and the bank was paying us exactly 15% interest, the Net Present Value is $0 (and not negative).

If the bank starts paying us more than 15% interest, then the Net Present Value will be positive. Hence, if the result is nil or positive, we will not lose money by investing in that project.

For multiple projects of similar risk and investment requirements, we would want to invest in a project with the highest Net Present Value, which in this case would be the bank.

So far, we have assumed that the investment is for three years only.

However, businesses have going concerns; that is to say, companies are expected to last indefinitely. As such, the cash inflows are supposed to be indefinite as well.

Therefore, under this circumstance, how do we find the Net Present Value of infinite cash inflows?

So let us modify our earlier proposed project slightly. Instead of projecting that cash flows will stop after Year 3, what if we become more realistic and assume that the business will continue indefinitely and will yield a profit of $3,000 in Year 4 and every year after that?

We might think about selling the company in Year 5, but that should not matter to our calculation because the price we will get for the business when we sell it should theoretically be equal to the present value (at the time of selling) of all future cash flows that can be expected from the business.

Now we have another challenge of finding the present value of hundreds (or thousands or even more) of expected cash flows!

If we assume that the hundreds of cash flows will be in equal amounts and that our required rate of return remains the same, there is a surprisingly easy way of calculating the present values of all such cash flows.

Present values of indefinite cash flows of equal amount, the first of which starts one period (year) from now can be derived as follows:

> **Present Value of Indefinite Cash Flows = Cash Flow ÷ Required Rate**

To prove this point, let us assume that we deposited our $30,000 in the bank for an indefinite period and will keep on getting an interest of $4,500 (at 15%) every year indefinitely.

The present value, of all such cash flows of $4,500, should intuitively be $30,000 because that is what we have deposited in the bank!

Applying the above formula should also give us the same present value of $30,000 (=$4,500÷15%).

Equipped with this knowledge, now we can find the present value of an indefinite number of equal cash flows that could be expected from a business.

Let us focus again on the earlier modified example, where we assumed that the business would not cease in three years, but rather it would keep on generating $3,000 profit in Year 4 and every year after that.

The cash flows can now be tabulated as follows:

	Today	Year 1	Year 2	Year 3
Cash Flows	-$30,000	$9,000	$13,000	$15,000
Value of indefinite cash flows				$20,000
Total cash flows	-$30,000	$9,000	$13,000	$35,000
Present value today of the future cash flows	-$30,000	$7,826	$9,830	$23,013
Net Present Value	$10,669			

Let us take a closer look at the above table. The value of indefinite yearly cash flows of $3,000 starting from Year 4 and beyond is $20,000 (=$3,000÷15%) in Year 3.

This is to say that if we wanted to sell off this business at the end of Year 3 (after taking in the 15,000 profits for that year), we would want to sell it for no less than $20,000. Hence, the total cash flows in Year 3 can be restated as $35,000.

We then find the present value of all these cash flows; for example, the present value of $35,000 three years from now is equal to $23,013 [=$35,000 ÷ (1+15%)3].

Adding all the present values and taking away the initial investment, we get a Net Present Value of $10,669.

It is good to know that this is a positive figure now which implies that by investing in this project, we would be increasing our wealth by $10,669 immediately.

To put it slightly differently, investing in this project is like paying $30,000 with our left hand and straight away getting $41,669 (=$30,000+$10,669) in our right hand!

We will recap the project appraisal technique in a few steps below:

- The Net Present Value technique starts with projecting the expected cash flows (profits) from a business for all future periods (years).
- We then calculate the present values of all such cash flows based on the time value of money.

- We add all the cash flows and take away the initial investment; what remains is known as the Net Present Value.
- A project with a positive Net Present Value can be undertaken as this enhances the wealth of the investor.
- There are a few other similar techniques for evaluating projects; most of them employ the idea of the time value of money.

However, discussing other methods is beyond the scope of this book. Nonetheless, it may be noted that Net Present Value is one of the most important and widely used techniques of project evaluation.

6. Simulating the financial impacts of decision-making

In this chapter, we will attempt to raise your understanding of how different managerial decisions impact financially on the business. A set of decision-making scenarios across different business functions are presented, and the potential impacts are ascertained. In doing this we hope that it will become clearer for you as an entrepreneur what the impacts are of your decisions because, in the end, all the decisions in a business context have a financial impact.

are presented However, discussing other methods is beyond the scope of this book. Nonetheless, it may be noted that Net Present Value is one of the most important and widely used techniques of project evaluation.

First, let us look at the financial effects of decisions related to the premises of your company, such as building or adapting installations, and buying equipment and machinery - known as fixed or tangible assets – or intangible assets such as patents and/or licenses.

The following tables give you a direct insight into the scope of the more typical management decisions that you must make when starting a business, the effects that must be considered before you commit to each decision, and how it impacts the financial side of your business.

For a better understanding of how to read the tables, here is an example. For example, when buying equipment for the business you are making an investment decision. You may want to think thoroughly about the cost of the equipment and find different alternatives by obtaining quotes from different suppliers, whilst also considering other aspects related to what the equipment does, its efficiency, capacity, and after-sales service provided by the vendor.

You may also consider whether it is better to buy or just to rent the equipment, as the latter can be a better approach in the sense that if things don't turn out the way you expect the cost will cease to exist once you return it to the vendor, compared to if you buy it and have to sell it by yourself to the market.

Concerning the financial impact of these decisions, buying investment equipment of course affects the capital expenditure or the money that you need to have upfront (CAPEX) (hence the sign ↗), but can also increase the operational expenditures (OPEX) particularly if the equipment requires insurance and fixed maintenance (or variable), etc. On the other hand, every asset owned by the company is subject to financial depreciation which must also be considered as this will affect your net profits in the P&L.

Decisions concerning tangible and intangible assets

Decision	Effects to be considered beforehand	Impact
Buying Equipment/ machinery/ vehicles	• Purchase costs • The efficiency of the different types of equipment/machinery etc. • The life expectancy of the equipment • After-sales service • Capacity • Rent vs buy	↗ CAPEX ↗ Fixed costs ↗ Depreciation ↗ Variable costs (insurance, maintenance)

Decision	Effects to be considered beforehand	Impact
Buying, building or renovating premises	• Purchase costs • Space available vs required (capacity) • Rent vs buy	
Buying patents or licensing rights	• Purchase costs • Contractual rights, obligations, and terms • Exclusivity agreements	↗ CAPEX ↗ Fixed costs ↗ Depreciation ↗ Variable costs (licensing fees and commissions paid to the licensors)

The next table is about the most frequent decisions concerning the recruitment of human resources for your business.

Decisions concerning human resources

Decision	Effects to be considered beforehand	Impact
Recruiting human resources	• Recruitment vs outsourcing (contractors) • Recruitment cost • Time to recruit • Worker ability and motivation • Salary and other benefits • Career progression/ barriers to exit • Productivity • Cost of replacement • Capacity	↗ Fixed costs ↗ Variable costs
Training human resources	• Recruitment cost • Time to train • Worker ability • Effects on productivity • Training cost • Training methods • Productivity	

The next table is about the most frequent decisions concerning the marketing and sales functions.

Decisions concerning marketing and sales

Decision	Effects to be considered beforehand	Impact
Invest in a brand strategy and communication	<ul><li>Brand awareness</li><li>Customer demand</li><li>Effects on conversion</li></ul>	↗ Revenue ↗ Intangible assets, and therefore, ↗ depreciation ↗ CAPEX ↗ Fixed costs (annual fees agreed with providers) ↗ Variable costs (paid to service providers)
Product Pricing	<ul><li>Customer Demand (can either affect positively or negatively)</li><li>Product differentiation and competitiveness</li><li>Effects on conversion</li></ul>	Revenue (can either increase or decrease)
Discounts	<ul><li>Customer Demand</li><li>Margins</li><li>Differentiation/image</li><li>Effects on conversion</li></ul>	↘ Revenue
Promotion	<ul><li>Brand awareness</li><li>Promotional scale/size</li><li>Promotional costs</li><li>Promotional media</li><li>Promotional reach</li><li>Customer demand</li><li>Effects on conversion</li></ul>	↗ Revenue ↗ Fixed costs ↗ Variable costs
Sales Channels (online, resellers, agents, retail, wholesale, etc.)	<ul><li>Brand awareness</li><li>Customer demand</li><li>Relationships with partners</li><li>Sales costs</li><li>Credit terms to buyers</li><li>Commissions to resellers/agents</li></ul>	↗ Revenue ↗ Fixed costs ↗ Variable costs ↘ Cash flow (because of the commissions and terms of payments to resellers/agents)

The next table is about the most frequent decisions concerning business operations.

Decisions concerning operations

Decision	Effects to be considered beforehand	Impact
Purchasing/ choice of supplier	• Choice of supplier • Time to delivery • The capacity of the supplier • Discounts • Credit terms	↗ Variable costs ↘ Cash flow (because of the conditions and terms of buying)
Purchasing/ stock level	• Space for stock/ floor area/ warehousing, utilities, insurance, security • Production capacity • Order frequency • Order cost • Order size • The efficiency of the operations	↗ Fixed costs ↗ Variable costs ↘ Cash flows
Production	• Equipment costs • Maintenance costs • Capacity vs flexibility to increase or downsize in the future • Insource vs Outsource • Productivity (human resources) • Efficiency (equipment) • Effectiveness and quality • Space required/area	↗ Fixed costs ↗ Variable costs
Logistics	• Internal or outsourcing • Capacity • Efficiency • Response time • Variable costs • Fixed costs	

Quality	• Level of quality desired • Level of quality required by the market	
Research and Development	• Product performance • Research time • Resources for research (human resources, equipment, outsourcing) • Competitiveness • Differentiation • Speed to market • Productivity • Production costs • Efficiency (to produce)	↗ Fixed costs ↗ Variable costs ↗ Revenues

Finally, the next table is about the most frequent **financial decisions**.

Decision	Effects to be considered beforehand	Impact
Borrowing	• Amount to borrow • Interests paid • Term • Early repayment charges • Short-term loan/overdraft for managing cash flows • Long-term loan for investments	↗ Cash flow ↗ Debt
Credit control/ Accounts receivable 9from customers)	• Administration costs • Agency fees (costs of debt collecting companies)	Cash flow (may increase or decrease depending on the conditions given to the customers)
Accounts payable (to suppliers)	• Administration costs • Can be an alternative to borrowing in the short term	Cash flow (may increase or decrease depending on the conditions given to the suppliers)
Equity	• Amount to raise • Percentage of equity to sell • Benefits of new shareholders • Dividends • Valuation of the business	↗ Cash flow

7. Legal Structure of a business

This subsection provides just a cursory glance into the complexities related to the legal structure of a business and its name.

An in-depth discussion is beyond the scope of this book; wherever appropriate, assistance from experts is advised. We hope that readers can now choose a legal structure that is most suitable to their specific needs and situations.

While starting a business, the legal structure of the company is something that needs to be carefully thought about because the legal structure of the business might have a direct impact on various essential issues like the calculation and payment of tax, registration, raising capital, record-keeping, decision-making, and financial liabilities that the business owner may be subject to.

In some cases, individuals may already be in business with some implied legal structure without being aware of the legal structure!

This section deals with the legal structure of business specifically in the UK, but the structure in many countries can be expected to be generally similar.

In the UK, businesses mostly belong to one of the following three categories: sole traders; partnerships; and limited liability companies. We will discuss each of these categories, along with their pros and cons, in the following section.

Sole trader - Think of this as someone being self-employed. This is a business owned by one person, and that person can work on their own or also hire other people to work for him/her.

A sole trader business is the easiest one to set up. If an individual is self-employed and has earned more than the minimum threshold in a tax year[1], he/she needs to register for self-assessment with HMRC for tax purposes.

As a single individual owns it, most sole proprietorships operate at a relatively small scale; but some might be large as the sole owner can hire many more individuals as the business grows.

A sole trader is self-employed and is subject to income tax[2] on the earnings from the company. Sole proprietorship gives entrepreneurs the freedom to do what they would love to do and to be their boss, and this might also bring about a sense of accomplishment.

On the flip side, a sole trader would have unlimited liability, i.e. in the event of things going wrong and the business incurring losses, the entrepreneur may have to pay from their sources even if that means selling off their assets.

The owner - despite possibly being smart - may not have ALL the skill sets necessary to run a successful business in this competitive world. Plus, one person might find it challenging to raise initial capital to start a business.

---

[1] £1000 for the tax year ending 5 April 2018
[2] See https://www.gov.uk/income-tax-rates for current rates of income tax

Moreover, if the company needs to be sold for any reason, the sale or transfer of ownership might be difficult.

There are also going to be concerns related to the continuity of the business: who will take care of the business if the entrepreneur takes medical leave or if something even worse was to happen to them?

This also means traditional financing institutions (like banks) will be less likely to lend money for business purposes to sole traders, and a sole trader might find it difficult to hire people.

Partnership - A partnership is a voluntary association between two or more individuals with the motive of making a profit. Two or more people called partners own a partnership.

The partners share the responsibility of the business along with the gains but are individually responsible for paying income taxes on their share of the profits.

The partners can have a partnership agreement that defines various aspects of running the business along with the profit-sharing arrangement.

One of the partners chosen to be a nominated partner and hence would be responsible for registering the partnership (with HMRC) and submitting periodic returns for tax purposes.

Partners also should individually file their tax returns with HMRC for income tax purposes.

Partners can choose to be sleeping partners whereby they contribute the capital but do not take part in the active day-to-day management of the business.

Generally, partners also have unlimited liability (just like a sole proprietor) unless they choose to be a limited partner rather than a general partner. A partnership with limited partners is called Limited Partnership. Such partnerships must be registered with the Registrar of Companies.

Such limited partners benefit from not being liable for any debts above the level of capital they have invested, but they are not allowed to retrieve the money they invested and cannot make management decisions.

Business partnerships can help mitigate some of the concerns associated with a sole proprietorship. One could choose business partners based on various complementary skill sets they can bring to form a successful business.

This can also address concerns related to the continuity of business if one partner falls ill. Workloads can also be shared among the partners and raising initial capital can be comparatively easier when there is more than one individual to chip in.

Though two heads are better than one concerning idea generation and running a business, it can also mean more conflict.

Unlike in sole proprietorship where the proprietor is the sole decision-maker, a partnership may require inputs from various partners for deciding, and this has a higher possibility of leading to disagreements and conflicts among the partners.

The nuts and bolts of how the partnership is to be run and how the profit is to be shared can be customised in the partnership agreement.

If no partnership agreement has been drawn up, given situations (e.g. profit-sharing, winding down) are governed by the Partnership Act 1890[3] (or Limited Partnership Act 1907 in the case of Limited Liability Partnership).

Hence, it is best to have a written agreement drawn up by a lawyer or accountant to avoid problems later. Among other things, it should include:

- The capital is to be contributed by each partner.
- The profit/loss sharing ratio.
- The rate of interest paid on capital.
- The rate of interest charged on drawings.
- Salaries to be paid.
- Arrangements for admitting new partners.
- The procedures for the exit of a partner.

Limited liability company - This is like an artificial person created by law and exercising most of the rights of a real person created by one or more investors (called shareholders). This keeps the business legally separate from the individuals who own the business.

---

[3] https://www.legislation.gov.uk/ukpga/Vict/53-54/39/contents for the full text of Partnership Act 1890

All the initial shareholders sign a legal statement called a memorandum of association where they agree to start a business (company). The firm is registered with Companies House and has a limited liability which means that the maximum amount the firm can lose generally cannot be more than its capital.

This safeguards the owners from having to pay out from their sources (e.g. by selling their car and house!).

Limited liability companies are registered with the Companies House, and they also need to register for Corporation Tax[4], which is different to Income Tax. Such companies should have at least one shareholder and at least one director.

The Articles of Association serve as guidelines regarding how the company should be managed and controlled.

A limited liability company could be private or public. Private companies' shares are not traded publicly (e.g. on London Stock Exchange) and their names end in 'Limited' or 'Ltd.'. Public Limited Companies have their names ending in Plc. (or Inc. in the USA).

Understandably, Public Limited Companies have more strict disclosure requirements than private companies as they are publicly bought and sold, and the share prices can fluctuate quite a lot.

If a potential investor would rather not start their own business but want to own a business, they could buy a few shares of a publicly

---

[4] https://www.gov.uk/corporation-tax for details on Corporation Tax

traded company (like Facebook) and be one of the shareholders of that company.

One of the major benefits of setting up a limited liability company is that - as the name suggests - the shareholders have limited liability. Since the company is a legal entity, the owners do not risk losing anything more than what they have already invested in the company (unless the owners or the directors do something foolish in which case, they might be personally liable).

Companies also tend to have better access to capital as they tend to have specialised management and they are expected to last indefinitely even if one or few key members are no longer able to carry on.

The transfer of ownership is also relatively easy for a company; the Facebook shares bought earlier by an investor could be sold just as quickly (though they might lose or gain some money depending upon what the market price of the share is at the time of the selling).

A significant drawback of a company is that shareholders could potentially be taxed twice. The company first pays corporation tax out of its profits. What remains can be paid out to shareholders as dividends. When shareholders receive dividends from their company, they may have to pay income tax on that dividend as well[5].

An essential part of starting a business is the name itself. After all, when investors are about to fulfil their lifelong passion of being their boss or start a new venture with their friends, it would be a good idea

---

[5] In the UK, usually, income tax is attracted only on the portion of dividend that is more than £5,000 per year.

to give the business a name that would be recognised later in its own right.

Whatever the legal structure of the company, specific rules have to be followed while naming the business. Of course, the name should not be offensive and should have an appropriate suffix (like LLP, Pvt., or Plc.). However, it should also not be too like another business that might already be operating. For example, a gentleman by the name of Jel Singh had a convenience store and named it Singhsbury's, which sounds very similar to a more famous supermarket.

Sainsbury's took exception to it and reportedly threatened the owner with a lawsuit. So Mr Singh decided to change the name to Morrisinghs[6], but thankfully another retail giant Morrisons did not complain about the name. At any rate, trying to come up with a name based on an already established name (e.g. naming MacroSoft for a new IT company) might be a risky business.

The name of the business should also not contain words or expressions (without permission) that imply a connection to government or local authorities. For example, if investors plan to open a pub and name it Great Britain Pub! they will need to demonstrate that the company is pre-eminent or very substantial in its field because of the use of Great Britain in the name. Similarly, entrepreneurs would not want to use the words 'Accredited by' in the name without permission[7].

---

[6] See http://www.dailymail.co.uk/news/article-4639878/Singhsbury-s-convenience-shop-changes-Morrisinghs.html for more on this.

[7] See https://www.gov.uk/government/publications/incorporation-and-names for a list of sensitive words

8. Bibliography

Arroteia, N., 2020. Starting a Business: a Guide for Scientists. Startup Finance.

Arroteia, N. and Bhatta, B., 2018. The Secrets to the Profitable Startup. Startup Finance.

Aulet, B., 2017. Disciplined entrepreneurship workbook. John Wiley & Sons.

Brealey, R. A., Myers, S. C., & Marcus, A. J., 2010. Fundamentals of corporate finance 6th ed., Boston: McGraw-Hill/ Irwin.

Chesbrough, H., Vanhaverbeke, W. and West, J. eds., 2006. Open innovation: Researching a new paradigm. Oxford University Press on Demand.

Drury, C., 2015. Management and cost accounting 9th ed., Andover: Cengage Learning.

Kotler, P., 2012. Kotler on marketing. Simon and Schuster.

Pride, W. M., Hughes, R. J., & Kapoor, J. R., 2016. Foundations of business 5th ed., Boston: Cengage Learning.

Ries, E., 2011. The lean startup: How today's entrepreneurs use continuous innovation to create radically successful businesses. Currency.

Sangster, A. & Wood, F., 2015. Frank Wood's business accounting 1 13th ed., Harlow: Pearson Education.

Saunders, M.N. and Lewis, P., 2012. Doing research in business & management: An essential guide to planning your project. Pearson.

Warren, C., Reeve, J., & Duchac, J., 2016. Financial & Managerial Accounting 14th ed., Boston: Cengage Learning.

9. Remissive index

A

accelerators 27

accounting .. 3, 26, 29, 31, 35, 64, 88, 90, 123, 124

accounts payable 113

accounts receivable 113

B

bottom-up analysis 18, 20

branding 25

break-even analysis . 4, 38, 56, 59, 62, 64, 66, 68, 71

break-even point (BEP) 38, 53, 54, 55, 56, 57, 58, 59, 60, 61, 62, 63

budget ... 5, 71, 72, 73, 74, 78, 79, 80, 81, 82, 85, 87, 88, 89, 90, 91

budgeting 71, 79

business angel 28, 93

business model 4, 9, 10, 11, 29, 30, 59

business partner 11, 28

C

capital expenditures (CAPEX) 80, 84, 85, 91, 94, 108, 109, 110

cash balance 81, 83, 84, 90

cash flow 5, 31, 41, 80, 85, 86, 88, 101, 102, 103, 04, 105, 113

cash inflow 80, 81, 82, 83, 88, 100, 101, 102

cash outflow 83, 88, 90

channel 9, 13, 25, 68

competition 45, 46, 60

competitor.. 10, 17, 27, 42, 45, 46

contribution margin ...51, 55, 57, 58, 63

cost. 10, 18, 31, 32, 33, 34, 35, 37, 38, 40, 43, 50, 56, 59, 124

credit 111, 113

crowdsourcing 95

crowdfunding 95

customer 9, 10, 11, 12, 13, 14, 18, 19, 20, 27, 30, 35, 37, 39, 41, 42, 43, 44, 45 customer journey 9, 14, 17

D
direct cost......................33, 34, 36
dividend..................................114

E
equity 93, 114

F
fixed cost 33, 34, 35, 36, 37, 38, 39, 40, 50, 51, 53, 55, 56, 57, 58, 59, 60, 61, 63, 108, 109, 110, 111, 112

forecasting 15
funding......................5, 30, 91, 95
funds 38, 54, 56

H
human resources 22, 23, 109, 110, 112, 113

I
incubator 27

indirect cost 33, 34, 35
insourcing................................. 27
intangible....................... 107, 108
internal rate of return (IRR) 97

L
legal Structure......................... 115
limited liability company....... 119
logistics............................. 26, 112

M
margin.......4, 32, 46, 50, 51, 59, 60
market research....... 12, 18, 25, 28
market segment 12, 19, 30
market share................. 17, 20, 73
market size 15, 16, 17, 21, 59
marketing................ 12, 22, 26, 42

N
net present value (NPV) . 97, 100, 101, 102, 104, 105, 107

O
operating expenditure 85

operating margin 51

operational profits 31

operations.. 22, 25, 32, 38, 41, 72, 80, 85, 94, 111, 112

operational expenditure (OPEX) 85, 91, 94, 108

outsourcing 27

overheads 34, 35, 78

P

profit and loss statement (P&L) 71, 87, 88, 89, 90, 108

payback 97

present value . 100, 101, 102, 103, 104

pricing . 25, 41, 42, 43, 44, 45, 46, 110

production 26, 34, 36, 43, 74, 112, 113

productivity .... 109, 110, 112, 113profit.............. 32, 53, 63, 87

profitability ... 3, 4, 29, 30, 31, 32, 50, 54, 62, 87

purchasing 25, 111, 112

Q

quality 26, 112

R

research and development 113

revenue 31, 32, 41, 110, 111

S

serviceable available market (SAM) 20, 21

serviceable obtainable market (SOM) 21

simulating 56, 59, 107

sole trader 116

supplier 11, 21, 26, 27, 40

T

total addressable market (TAM) 17, 18, 20, 21

tangible 19, 107, 108

top down analysis 18, 19

V

valuation 5, 94, 95, 114

value proposition 9, 11, 14, 18, 24, 25, 34

variable cost 34, 36, 37, 38, 39, 40, 43, 50, 51, 53, 54, 57, 58, 60, 108, 109, 110, 111, 112

variable margin 50, 51

venture capital 93

Another title from the same authors

www.ingramcontent.com/pod-product-compliance
Lightning Source LLC
Chambersburg PA
CBHW050012230526
45465CB00003BB/1385